Report Builder & Report Models in Microsoft SQL Server 2005

Insight in Structure, Usage and Best Practices

DI Gerald Schinagl

namo thassa bhagavato arahato samma sambuddhasa

Thanks for all the beings that made this book possible

Kevin Cox (Microsoft SQLCAT Team)

Companies spend a lot of money collecting data and it is important to have the right tools available to extract information from that data. Many companies have a large backlog of work in the IT department, so the business departments are seeking tools and techniques to empower their employees to be more self sufficient.

Giving Information Workers the ability to create their own reports is an important strategy for Microsoft. SQL Server 2005 and the upcoming SQL Server 2008 will come with the Report Builder and Report Designer tools. Microsoft Office 2007 also has a greatly enhanced set of features for working with data. These tools cover a broad range of reports – from scheduled reports to ad-hoc queries and many more.

Gerald has written this book to give you the best tips and techniques for getting the most out of Report Builder. He has spent some time explaining the importance of report models and understanding your data.

Enjoy your reading!

Dear valued readers

Some time ago I was pushing Microsoft for more and more documentation and information about the internals of Report Models. At this time I thought that for sure someone will write a book about this new featureset of SQL Server 2005. But time went by and no book appeared on the market.

As I was not satisfied with the information floating around I decided to write a book on that them to spread the knowledge I got and deliver a Manual for development and training purposes. This approach was encouraged by Carolyn Chau (Senior Program Manager for Report Builder) so I stated off and now, some months later the book you hold in your hands is finished.

My thanks go to Carolyn Chau, Bob Meyers, Kevin Cox, Mike Kilpatrick for supporting me in technical issues as well as in proof – reading the manuscript.

A big Thanks goes to my wife who gave me the time to write this book and supported me in doing my first book ever.

November 2007

Gerald Schinagl

Table of Contents

1 WELCOME TO REPORT MODELS & REPORT BUILDER 10

    1.1 What is Report Builder 10
    1.2 A short Report Builder History 12
    1.3 How this book is organized 13
    1.4 The sample project(s) 14

2 SETTING UP REPORT BUILDER & THE WORKING ENVIRONMENT 15

    2.1 Installing and configuring Reporting Services 15
    2.2 Configuring the Reporting Services environment for the usage of Report Builder 16
    2.3 Setting up your Report Model development environment 17
    2.4 Where is everything? 18
        2.4.1 Working with Report Models 19
        2.4.2 Use Report Builder 20

3 GENERATING YOUR FIRST REPORT MODEL 22

    3.1 Generating a Report Model on relational data using Model Designer .. 22
    3.2 Generating a Report Model on a multidimensional database using SQL Server Management Studio 30

4 THE INTERNAL STRUCTURE OF A REPORT MODEL 32

    4.1 The Semantic Model object 34
        4.1.1 ID 34
        4.1.2 Description: 34
        4.1.3 Version 35
        4.1.4 Culture 35
        4.1.5 DataSource View 37
        4.1.6 Namespace Prefixes 37
        4.1.7 Folder (EntityFolder) 38
        4.1.8 Custom Properties 40
        4.1.9 Perspectives 40
    4.2 Entities 42
        4.2.1 ID 44
        4.2.2 Name 44
        4.2.3 Description 45
        4.2.4 Collection Name 45

- 4.2.5 IdentifyingAttributes 45
- 4.2.6 DefaultDetailAttributes 46
- 4.2.7 DefaultAggregate Attributes 47
- 4.2.8 Sort Attributes 47
- 4.2.9 InstanceSelection 48
- 4.2.10 IsLookup 49
- 4.2.11 Inheritence 51
- 4.2.12 Disjoint Inheritance 53
- 4.2.13 Fields 53
- 4.2.14 Binding 53
- 4.2.15 SecurityFilter 54
- 4.2.16 Default Security Filter 55
- 4.2.17 Hidden 55
- 4.2.18 Custom Properties 56
- 4.3 FIELDS 56
- 4.4 ATTRIBUTES 56
  - 4.4.1 ID 57
  - 4.4.2 Name 57
  - 4.4.3 Description 58
  - 4.4.4 Alignment 58
  - 4.4.5 DataType 58
  - 4.4.6 Nullable 62
  - 4.4.7 Expression 62
  - 4.4.8 SortDirection 62
  - 4.4.9 Width 63
  - 4.4.10 MimeType 63
  - 4.4.11 DataCulture 64
  - 4.4.12 DiscourageGrouping 64
  - 4.4.13 EnableDrilltrough 64
  - 4.4.14 Format 65
  - 4.4.15 ContextualName 65
  - 4.4.16 IsAggregate 65
  - 4.4.17 IsFilter 66
  - 4.4.18 OmitSecurityFilters 66
  - 4.4.19 ValueSelection 66
  - 4.4.20 Binding 67
  - 4.4.21 Default Aggregate Attribute 67
- 4.5 ROLES 68
  - 4.5.1 ID 68
  - 4.5.2 Name 68
  - 4.5.3 Description 68

	4.5.4	Linguistics	68
	4.5.5	RelatedRoleID	69
	4.5.6	Cardinality	69
	4.5.7	ContextualName	70
	4.5.8	HiddenFields	70
	4.5.9	ExpandInline	71
	4.5.10	PromoteLookup	71
	4.5.11	Preferred	72
	4.5.12	Recursion	72
	4.5.13	Binding	72
	4.5.14	Hidden	72
4.6	FILTERS		73
4.7	EXPRESSIONS		73
	4.7.1	Expression Builder GUI	73
	4.7.2	Report Functions	76
4.8	EVOLVING YOUR REPORT MODEL OVER TIME		84
4.9	PUBLISHING A REPORT MODEL		86
	4.9.1	Build a Report Model Project	86
	4.9.2	Deploy a Report Model	86
	4.9.3	Associate a Report Model with a DataSource	88
5	**GENERATING YOUR FIRST AD HOC REPORT IN 5 MINUTES**		**89**
6	**THE REPORT BUILDER CLIENT**		**92**
6.1	STARTING THE APPLICATION		92
6.2	WHERE DOES REPORT BUILDER GET ITS INFO FROM?		93
6.3	DATA AND NAVIGATION IN REPORT BUILDER		94
	6.3.1	Report Builder Fields	94
	6.3.2	Report Builder Navigation	95
6.4	CREATING AND EDITING A REPORT		100
	6.4.1	Report Templates	101
	6.4.2	General Report Properties	102
	6.4.3	Page Properties (Page Layout)	103
6.5	DESIGNING A REPORT		104
	6.5.1	Titlebox, Filterbox and Row Count	104
	6.5.2	Report Background	105
	6.5.3	Images	105
	6.5.4	Textbox	106
	6.5.5	Executing, exporting and printing a Report	107
	6.5.6	Rendering considerations	107
	6.5.7	Formatting basics for Textboxes, Rows, Columns and Cells	110

- 6.5.8 Generating List and Matrix Reports 111
- 6.5.9 Graphical Reports (Charts) 113
- 6.6 FORMULAS AND CALCULATED FIELDS 119
- 6.7 FILTERING DATA 120
  - 6.7.1 Filtergroups and complex filters 124
  - 6.7.2 Filtering and Formulas 125
  - 6.7.3 Filtering at runtime 126
  - 6.7.4 Prefiltered Lists 127
- 6.8 GROUPING 128
- 6.9 SORTING 129
- 6.10 CLICKTHROUGH REPORTS (AKA AS INFINITE DRILL-TROUGH REPORTING) 130
  - 6.10.1 Temporary drill-trough Reports 130
  - 6.10.2 Predefined (static) drill-trough Reports 131
- 6.11 PUBLISH REPORTS 131

7 SECURITY 133

- 7.1 REPORT MODEL SECURITY 133
- 7.2 REPORT BUILDER CLIENT SECURITY 136
  - 7.2.1 Report Builder Role 137
  - 7.2.2 Model Item Browser Role 138

8 REPORT MANAGEMENT 139

- 8.1 THE REPORTING SERVICES WEBSERVICE 139
- 8.2 THE REPORTING SERVICES DATABASE 141
  - 8.2.1 Database – Tables 142
  - 8.2.2 Used stored procedures 143
- 8.3 TRANSFORMATION OF REPORT BUILDER REPORTS TO REPORT DESIGNER REPORTS 146
- 8.4 SUBSCRIPTION 146
- 8.5 BUILDING REPORT DESIGNER REPORTS ON A REPORT MODEL DATASOURCE 146
- 8.6 EDITING A REPORT DESIGNER – REPORT IN REPORT BUILDER 147

9 TIPS & TRICKS 148

- 9.1 REPORT MODEL TRICKS 148
  - 9.1.1 Version Management & other Metadata 148
  - 9.1.2 Calculated fields 149
  - 9.1.3 Handling intersection Table (or how to handle m:n relationships) 149
  - 9.1.4 Handling the MultiRoles Problem 151
  - 9.1.5 Evaluating the group – membership of a Report user 152
  - 9.1.6 The generated SQL/MDX Code of the Report Model Engine 153

9.2 REPORT BUILDER CLIENT TRICKS 154
   9.2.1 Launching Report Builder from a custom application 154
   9.2.2 Enhancing the Report during publishing 156
   9.2.3 Retrieving images that are not inside the database................. 156
   9.2.4 Using RDL expressions in Report Builder 156
9.3 REPORT MANAGEMENT TRICKS 157
   9.3.1 Building a Report Model on a Reporting Server Database 157
   9.3.2 Using Visual Studio 200 Team Edition to Stress test your Report Server 158

1 Welcome to Report Models & Report Builder

1.1 What is Report Builder

Report Builder is a new kid on the block of the Microsoft SQL Server 2005 ecosystem. Report Builder is contained in the Reporting Services stack and enhances the functionality of Reporting Services 2005.

> **Note:** The term Report Builder is used by Microsoft to describe the infrastructure that provides the capabilities for ad hoc reporting. The client application carries (at least in this edition of SQL Server) the same name. To distinguish these two the infrastructure is referred to as Report Builder in this book whereas Report Builder client stands for the application to design the ad hoc reports.

The solution consists of two parts, that rely integral on each other and leverage the security, storage and management capabilities of Reporting Services.

- **Report Model:** This structure acts as an abstraction layer to the underlying database (relational databases as well as multidimensional databases like OLAP cubes or UDM structures). A Report Model is the business description of the data contained in the abstracted DataSource and hides the complexity of the possible large and technically optimized database schema from the Information workers, making it easier for them to accomplish the task of creating ad hoc Reports using Report Builder. Besides a user friendly naming of objects, this structure bears a lot of built in intelligence to hide complexity from the designated user and defines the universe he or she can create an ad - hoc Report later on. A Report Model has to be designed by a developer in Visual Studio 2005 (or higher) or Business Intelligence Studio 2005 (or higher) and needs to be deployed to a Reporting Server to be available for Report Builder for defining Reports based on it. I will show some tricks later on, which make the life for the Information workers easier and enhance the usability of the provided data through the Report Model over the boundaries Microsoft provides out of the box.

- **Report Builder client:** Is an ad hoc Reporting tool contained in SQL Server 2005 that leverages the information, abstraction and metadata that is contained in a Report Model and allows the Information worker to define Reports by himself without the demand for a developer, which is also known as *ad Hoc Reporting* or *self-service Reporting*. The definition of the information a user of Report Builder needed, together with the metadata contained in the Report Model yields a set of queries that are executed against the database (aka as Semantic Query) the Report Model is built on. The styling of the Report Builder application is similar to the style of Microsoft Office 2003, so the people who usually use Microsoft Excel 2003 for their work get familiar with the tool in a short amount of time.

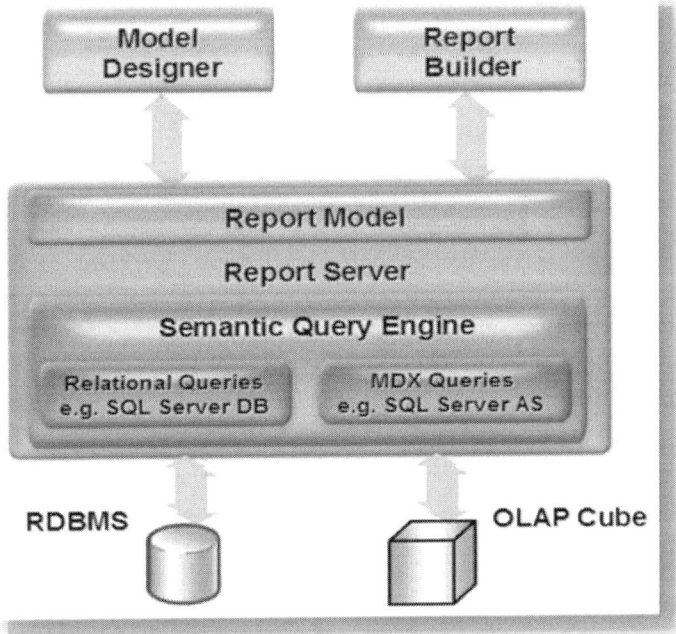

Image 1: Schema of Report Builder Components

1.2 A short Report Builder History

In April 2004 Microsoft acquired a company called Active Views whose founders had developed a toolset that, over an abstraction layer, allowed end users to generate their own reports against relational databases without knowing about Tables, Views, and Constraints of the targeted data source.

The ideas and concepts of this product were taken, reviewed, re-architected and integrated into the Business Intelligence - stack of SQL Server 2005. This piece of software was positioned as the missing link to provide self-defined reporting for information workers that was absent and missing since the introduction of Reporting Services for SQL Server 2000. Reporting Services 2000 was already a very powerful solution but still needed developers to create the Report in Visual Studio which is a caveat in some scenarios in terms of usability, flexibility and costs. For this reason some third party products were built that gave users an easy way to layout their reports outside of Visual Studio. But these solutions still required the person who built the report to have a great knowledge of the structure and relations of the database they were working on so there was still demand for a solution that keeps the Information worker in focus.

Report Models, which were introduced by Microsoft, deliver an abstraction layer for the Information Worker aside from Tables, Columns and Procedures. The targeted user of the ad hoc Report tool defines his or her queries in objects he or she knows from their business without any needed knowledge about the underlying database structures, exaggerated spoken the Information worker does not even need to know whether the information he or she retrieves resides in a relational database or an OLAP cube.

When executing the semantic query that results out of the Report Model it is translated into a set of T-SQL queries or MDX queries in case the data source is a UDM/OLAP Cube by the Reporting Services Semantic Query Engine using the Report Models metadata. These queries extract the data out of the source systems as needed and combine them before presenting the collected data to the user.

1.3 How this book is organized

This book is not an *"I will tell you how to define a Report Model in 127 Steps Book"*. It does not describe every basic concept of Reporting Services or Analysis Services as I assume the reader should have some basic knowledge or acquire the knowledge consulting other books or the internet in the fields of the Microsoft Business Intelligence stack and some basic knowledge of .NET programming. I just want to give you, the reader, the new and needed information in a more descriptive way, and don't want to repeat information other authors have already perfectly described in their books.

This book describes a lot of scenarios and features using small samples and/or images when needed but require you to build your own solutions based on the surrounding conditions and limitations of your scenario.

The chapters of the book target different audiences. Depending on the distribution of responsibilities in a company the one or other chapter might apply to different audiences. Also keep in mind that due to the logical integral connection of the Report Builder´s modules the information is interwoven and in some places can`t be separated absolutely into chapters, so also a chapter for which you are not the primary targeted audience might be worth reading as it contains some information or link you might be looking for.

In the rest of the book I will refer to four different Roles or Audiences, which I will describe in brief in this place:

- **Developer:** This is the person who designs a Report Model. He has to know the source-systems and their specific capabilities and uses Business Intelligence Studio 2005 or Visual Studio 2005 to generate, modify and deploy the Report Models.
- **Administrator**: This person, usually the DBA of the Reporting Server Database is the one who maintains that the systems are up and running, monitors for bottlenecks and manages permissions and security settings. It is depending on company policy who of these first two Roles is allowed to publish a Report Model to the Report Server. The typical toolset of the administrator is SQL Server Management Studio and the Report Manager.

- **Information worker:** This person is the targeted user of the ad hoc Reporting tool to generate reports based on the Report Model a developer has previously created and deployed. This person, who usually does not need to have a deep technical background (e.g. a Power user) creates the Reports and can save them in his own environment first. If he or she also has the permission to publish Reports to the Report Server for a shared consumption is depending on companies policies. The toolset this Role works with is the Report Builder client application.
- **End user:** The last point in our chain this is the person who consumes the generated Reports via Web browser or a custom application. The only interaction he or she has with the system is to provide selections the Information worker has designed. For the end user it does not make any difference how the Report he or she consumes was designed, weather it originated out of Report Designer as a Standard Report or Report Builder.

Chapter 2 tells you how to set up the system and targets the administrator of the Report Server. The Chapters 3 and 4 deal with the generation, modification and management of a Report Model, which is usually the job of a developer. Chapter 5 describes the usage of the Report Builder Client and is centred on the Information worker and of course his/her support stuff. Chapters 6 to 8 deal with administrative and architectural stuff and apply for developers as well as for administrators. Finally Chapter 9 points out some interesting tips and tricks that ease the live for all audiences.

1.4 The sample project(s)

The samples used in this book are based on the AdventureWorks and AdventureworksDW Database, which is are the sample databases Microsoft delivers in SQL Server 2005. If a sample is built on other structures they will be accessible from the book´s CD/Website.

2 Setting up Report Builder & the working environment

As Report Builder & Report Models are a part of Reporting Services 2005[1] the server – based components are set up with Reporting Services, whereas the Report Builder Client is downloaded from this Reporting Server on demand to the local client and cached on the machine where it is executed. This process is described in chapter 6.1.

2.1 Installing and configuring Reporting Services

To install the needed components on a server run the SQL Server Installation Wizard to set up a default configuration or a files-only configuration. A default configuration installs all components of Reporting Services on a single server. This installation option is only available if you are installing the Database Engine (for the Reporting Services databases) and Reporting Services at the same time. A files-only installation copies the needed files to disk and minimally configures the Report Server. After the setup is completed, you have to use the Reporting Services Configuration tool to customise the settings (for example point reporting Services to a specific database Server where the reporting Services databases are located) and bring the Report Server online. This approach allows you to specify remote computers (for example, choosing a remote Database Engine instance to host the report server databases), or deploy Reporting Services on distributed servers, scale-out deployment, or on Internet-facing Web servers. Further Information about the setup and configuration can be accessed on the MSDN-Website on a general level http://msdn2.microsoft.com/en-us/library/ms143736.aspx or specific for a one-machine-setup on http://msdn2.microsoft.com/en-us/library/ms144290.aspx)

---

[1] Reporting Services is contained in SQL Server 2005 Enterprise, Standard and Workgroup edition. In the Workgroup – Edition there are some limitations on the possible DataSources that can be used. The Enterprise edition is the only edition that allows infinite Click trough Reports (see 6.10)

For more information about setup, configuration and other topics on the Business Intelligence components of SQL Server 2005 please refer to Delivering Business Intelligence with Microsoft SQL Server 2005 from Brian Larson (ISBN 0-07-226090-4) or Reporting Services from Michael Lisin and Jim Joseph (ISBN 0-672-32799-6).

2.2 Configuring the Reporting Services environment for the usage of Report Builder

Once Reporting Services is installed and working properly on your server; you have to open up your mind for some specific settings affecting Report Builder client besides the classic settings for Reporting Services which I will not refer to in this book. The most important decision is the kind of authentication you will need to give the targeted users' access to the Report Builder Client.

- Authentication is easy, if there is a **trust relationship** between the Reporting Server and the used Domain account to access Report Builder (using Windows Authentication), which is usually the case. Both – the Server and the Domain account used to access the application are contained in the same Domain or in two Domains that trust each other. In that case just make sure that Windows Authentication is enabled on the virtual folder of Internet Information Services where your Report Builder application (usually http://yourserver/reportserver/) is contained. As the credentials of the active user who executes Report Builder client are immediately handed over for authentication it seems seamless for the information worker, who is using Report Builder client and gives him or her single sign on (SSO) experience.

- For users who have to use **stored credentials** (Forms Authentication) on the client for the authentication against Report Server, (for example the *Remember my password* checkbox in Internet Explorer) you have to make sure those credentials are registered as Windows credentials on the Reporting Server (either as Domain Accounts or Local Accounts) otherwise Report Builder cannot be executed.

Also Basic Authentication needs to be enabled on the Report Builder folder in Internet Information Services (IIS). From a security perspective this option is only recommended if you are using SSL to secure the transport layer and only if the corporate guidelines allow users to locally store their credentials (which happens in that case). If no credentials are stored, the Report Builder application´s download will simply fail. Different then for example Internet Explorer the users will not be prompted to supply any additional credentials.

- The least recommended option is to have **anonymous access** enabled on your Internet Information Services – Report Builder Folder. Be aware that this approach makes your server vulnerable to a bunch of attacks, so think twice if you really want to take the risks or if there is another way to define an authentication – schema for your demand.

Standard Report Builder Access is enabled after you installed reporting Services. If for any reason you want to disable the download of Report Builder client the *EnableReportDesignClientDownload* has to set to false using scripts (for the usage of scripts on Reporting Services refer to Books Online).

2.3 Setting up your Report Model development environment

There are a lot of tools you might need or use to work with a Report Model in the one or other way, depending on your Roles in the development process. The clarification about the component usage for different purpose will be delivered later on. In this place I will just outline how to set up the individual pieces of software:

- **Visual Studio:** If there is an installation of Visual Studio (at least 2005) on the targeted client, where Report Models are to be developed the collection of available projects (templates) will be enhanced to also contain all templates of business intelligence projects. One of these templates is the Report Model Project that contains the *Model Designer* plug in.

- **Business Intelligence Studio 2005:** This application, which is targeted for all kinds of development in the Business Intelligence section (SSIS, SSAS, SSRS), is installed during the setup of the client side components if there is no Visual Studio installed on the targeted client. Business Intelligence Studio is a stripped down version of Visual Studio that just provides the templates mentioned above. One of these templates is the Report Model Project that contains the *Model Designer* plug in.
- **SQL Server Management Studio:** This application, which is the main tool for management and administration in SQL Server 2005, is installed with the client side components and allows doing the administrative tasks on a Reporting Services Server.
- **Report Manager:** The Report Manager Website is a component that is installed with the server based components of Reporting services and is installed with these components already. Report Manager is the standard-web interface for management and consumption of Reports as well as the starting point to get Report Builder downloaded to the local client.

2.4 Where is everything?

As there are several components working together in an integral way when using the Report Builder infrastructure you might be confused which piece of the solution is located in which place and plays which Role in the concert. The following two diagrams give an impression where the structures that this book covers are located and how they interact on a general level with each other.

2.4.1 Working with Report Models

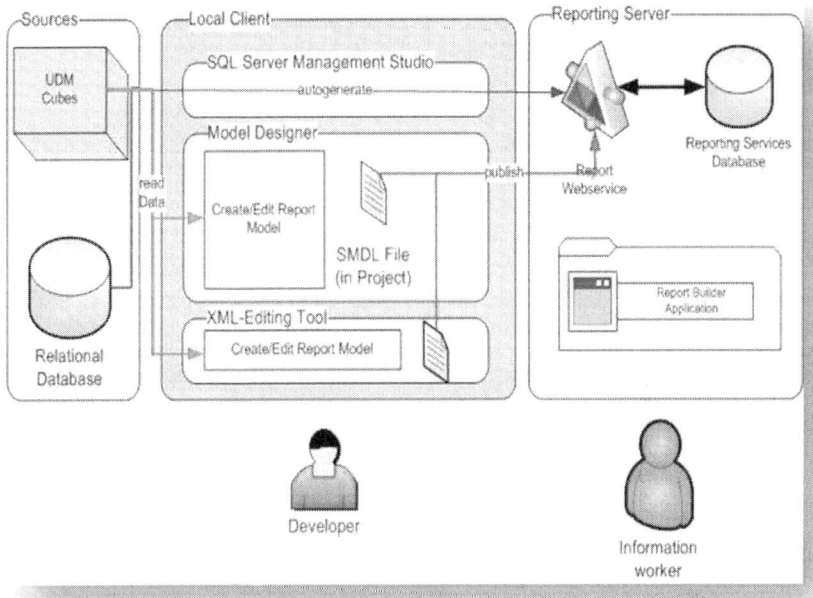

Image 2: Structural Schema for Report Model generation

The Report Model is the starting point to generate ad hoc Reports using Report Builder. As I will point out in the following chapters you will see that each Report, designed in Report Builder is based on a Report Model as its DataSource. Therefore first a Report Model has to be created. The labour on a Report Model is done on the local client of a developer, using the information contained in the source databases that have to be accessible at least during the initial generation of the Report Model. If you are using SQL Server Management Studio to execute this job, the Report Model is generated and published to the Report Server on the fly using the Report Server´s Webservice without a possibility to change the rules by which the Report Model is designed or to save and edit the generated Report Model.

If you define and edit your Report Model in Model Designer, you are creating a Visual Studio Project that contains the

DataSource View Files, the SMDL Models and some project – metadata files. When deploying the Report Model to the Report Server the information contained in the DataSource View is merged into the SMDL file (and also published on the Report Server in this way).

The last option is to build the SMDL - file on your own using an XML - editing tool or a custom application and publish it to the Report Server using the Webservice, although this approach is not recommended by Microsoft.

The Report Server consists of the already mentioned Webservice and the Report Server Database which will be covered in chapter 8.1. On the Report Server there are no SMDL - files stored; the information contained in these files is transferred into the Reporting Server Database which is also known as Catalogue into a binary representation.

The Report Server also carries a virtual directory in IIS, where the Report Builder Application can be downloaded from by the information worker who wants to create or modify a report.

2.4.2 Use Report Builder

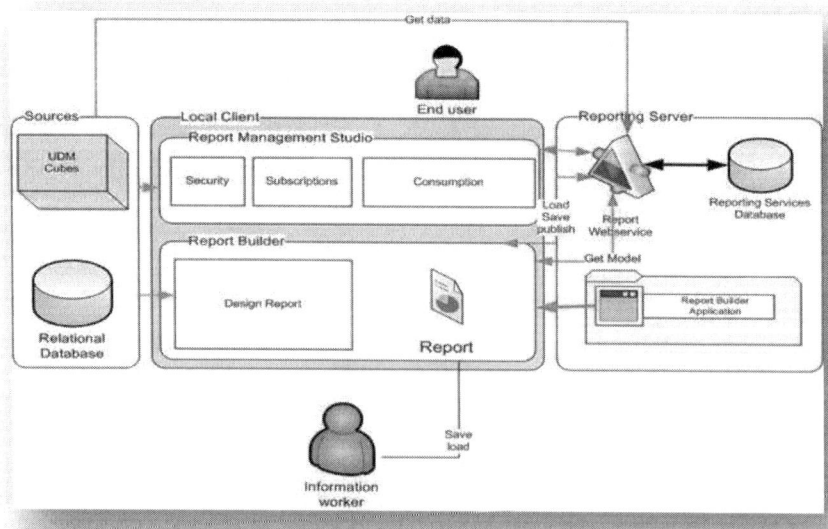

Image 3: Structural Schema for Report Builder usage

The first step an Information worker needs to accomplish, when dealing with ad hoc Reports is to start the according application. This is either already cached on the local Client or will be downloaded from a Report Server and then start as a Windows Client application (aka as SmartClient).

Once Report Builder client is started it contacts its associated Reporting Server (that is the Server where it was downloaded from) to get a list of available Report Models to work with. This list is presented to the user as the first choice to choose from when creating a new report. With SP2 of SQL Server 2005 you also have the possibility to choose other report Servers to retrieve a Report Model from (see Chapter 6.2)

After the selection of a template how the Report should look like (available are Table, Matrix or Chart) you can define which objects you want to use in the Report and how it should be filtered, grouped and layouted. From time to time you may want to check in the preview-mode how the report looks like using live data – for that purpose the source database is contacted. At every point the report definition can be saved either on the file system of the local client or at the Reporting Server. Finally the Report is published to the Report Server using the Webservice and will be available for the users either trough the means of the Reporting Portal (Report Manager) or other access.

3 Generating your first Report Model

The Report Model (also referred to as Semantic Model in some publications) is stored as an XML - file whose definitions and information are the origin for the construction of user defined Reports in Report Builder. The Report Model acts as an abstraction and enhancement layer to the underlying database to hide the complexity of the sources from the users of Report Builder and provide an enhanced user experience compared to other approaches to generate ad hoc Reports.

In this part of the book I will take you through the process of the creation and maintenance of a Report Model, based on SQL Server 2005 on the fast track.

3.1 Generating a Report Model on relational data using Model Designer

If the Report Model that is being designed is to be based on relational data the developer has to use Model Designer (which is contained in Business Intelligence Studio or Visual Studio) as the primary tool to create, edit and maintain the Report Model. Remember - if the Report Model is generated using SQL Server 2005 Management Studio it is created and published to the Report Server on the fly and cannot be modified any more with the tools Microsoft provides at the moment, in this case you have to take the Report Model as it is. If you really want to give your Information workers all the power and usability a Report Model bears I do absolute recommend using Model Designer as your tool of choice.

To generate a Report Model in Model Designer first there has to be a Report Model Project created. Besides the content-files that will be described later on and the compulsive Solution - Files (like in any other Visual Studio Solution) Business Intelligence Studio or Visual Studio created two Report - Model project related files of specific interest:

- **Projectname.smdlproj**: In that configuration - file Model Designer stores some user related settings like the compile and deployment specifications as well as encrypted credentials for UserIds and passwords if the designer provided them.

- **Projectname.database**: First of all don't be baffled that the file type may be associated with Microsoft Analysis Services on your local client as the standard application to edit it. In reality, if you open the file with any text editor you will recognise it is just another XML – file. This is a file where Model Designer obviously tracks what has happened to the main objects in the project (last updates of the schema, last processing of the Report Model, state of deployment, etc) so it might be interesting to extract some of this information if you are required to keep track of changes in that layer, for example for compliance reasons. One word of caution in this place – do not open and modify this file in Business Intelligence Studio 2005 or Visual Studio 2005 using the default GUI these tools recommend– as to the file type, in that case an interface for a real database file is presented that will destroy the structure of the file if you save the contents.

After the project is successfully created, the next step to take for you as a developer is to define at least one data source. Keep in mind that right now you can only use Microsoft SQL Server 2005 or 2000 as a source for Report Models as the Semantic Query Engine is not yet defined for other databases, but with SP2 of Microsoft SQL Server it is also be the possible to use Oracle version 9.2.0.3 and up as a source database[2]. It is a good practice I recommend in this place, to use the correct server name when defining the connection properties in the data source, instead of localhost or . (dot) as you might end up with problems during the deployment phase in some special circumstances when the source database server is not named fully qualified.

With this release of SQL Server it is also not possible to use a Custom DataSource (that works using Reporting Services) as a data source for a Report Model.

Based on the defined data source you have to create at least one Data Source View in the following step. This is a

---

[2] Keep in mind that you need the Oracle Client installed on both, the Reporting Server as well as on the Client where Report Builder is executed to work correctly.

structure where the developer defines which of the (probably) many Tables or Views of the underlying database may be used in the Report Model, like you do it in other Business Intelligence Projects. In the DataSource View only the Entity's you will really need in the Report Model later, either as a real Entity or a Lookup should be contained to keep the list of objects to work with as narrow as possible. In a Data Source View you can use Tables, Views or Named Queries[3] as a source of data. Unfortunately it is not possible to add System Tables or System Views to the Data Source View in the Designer (and it would not help you to add them by tweaking the file as System Objects are omitted in Model generation later on). So if you want or have to build a Report Model on the Metadata of SQL Server 2005 you have to expose these Objects either as a View or use Named Queries and define logical primary keys in the DSV where they are missing. A Report Model for this purpose is described later on in the Tips & Tricks section. If you have a large relational Database and want to pre-limit the number of objects that are presented by the wizard to be contained in the DSV, you can use the *Advanced Data View Options* to restrict the list of the available objects to select from by schema-names you can provide.

The DataSource View is the place where you can enhance the existing Entities (out of the database) with calculated fields (using T-SQL) and do some cleansing in the naming of Tables and Columns so the later on generated Report Models won´t need that much tweaking to show nice, user-friendly names.

If you intent to use your DataSource View to target different databases of the same schema - for example when programming against a test-system and later using the Report Model on the production system, you will have to open the DataSource View-file (it is an XML file with the ending .dsv) with a XML - editor and remove the schema

---

[3] A Named Query is the means how you can bring the output of a Table-valued Function or a SQLCLR Function with a returning Table into the DataSource view. But keep in mind that in this release of the product you cannot set parameters dynamically, you have to provide them a fixed value during the definition of the Named Query.

prefixes that Business Intelligence Studio or Visual Studio put in, as these tools are always using full qualified object names. Removing the database-qualifier enables the Semantic Query engine to access different databases as long as they bear to the same schema. But don't forget – as the Semantic Queries are built using the databases metadata (at design time !), the databases used for the Report Model creation and the usage of the Report Model afterwards should not differ too much in their fill factors to earn an appealing query performance.

Existing references (foreign keys) between Tables are derived from the underlying DataSource and shown in DSV Designer, but there is also the possibility to ad own references in that layer if there are some logical references missing in the underlying database. If the DataSource does not provide references by foreign keys and you are running on SQL Server 2005 Enterprise Edition the DSV Wizard will popup an additional screen that allows you to do a name-based matching of possible key columns, if you don't run this edition you have to define the relations yourself in the DSV-Designer surface without any additional support.

For more information on which properties you can modify in a DataSource View have a look at http://msdn2.microsoft.com/en-us/library/ms174778.aspx.

Finally you can start to generate the Report Model itself. This is done with a wizard, called the Report Model generation Wizard.

The Report Model generation uses a process called auto generation if you want to create your Model for the first time or refresh it in case the underlying schema has changed. It is your choice if you want to populate the initial Report Model with Entities, Attributes and Roles already or if you prefer to create an empty Report Model and add the objects piece by piece by yourself.

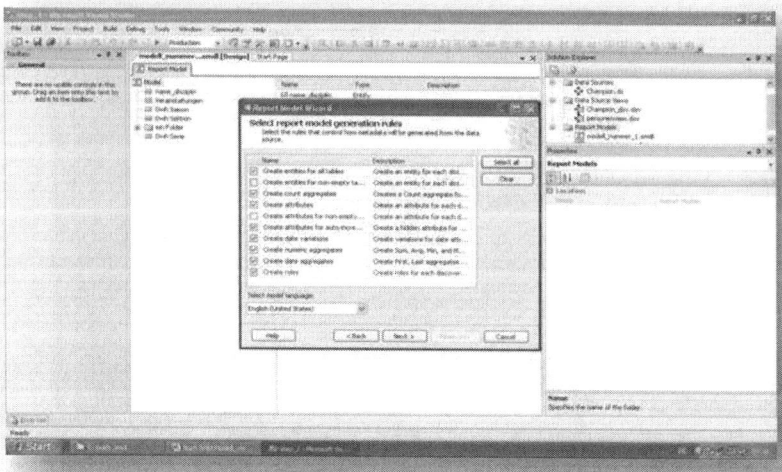

Image 4: Start page of the Report Model generation wizard

You are guided through the wizard, where you can define some specific settings (the wizard already gives some recommendations) in the first screen. These settings and other internal Rules that are defined in the file ReportModelgenerationRules.smgl[4] are taken into account when the Report Model is generated.

- **Create Entities for all Tables:** The definition of is this option is a bit misleading; if it is checked (which is the default), the Model Generation Engine generates an Entity for **each** according object (not just Tables but also Views and Named Queries) that is enclosed in the DataSource View and contains a Primary Key or a logical key.
- **Create Entities for non-empty Tables:** This option is an enhancement of the above one. If it is checked the Model Generation Engine only creates Entities for all

---

[4] This undocumented file contains the Rules the Report Model generation engine uses to define how the Report Model is generated. It is possible to tweak these rules but be aware that this is not supported by Microsoft and there is no assurance that the structure of this file will not change with a Service Pack.

objects in the DataSource View that contain at least one entry (one row of data) at the point in time when the Report Model is generated, and a Primary Key or a logical key is defined on the object in the DSV.

- **Create count aggregates:** If this option is checked the Report Model generation engine creates a Count - aggregate (#Entity stands for Number of Entities in the generated Report Model) for you. If you don´t need these aggregates in your Report Model uncheck the Box.
- **Create Attributes:** If the option is checked, for each appropriate Column in the already created Entities, an Attribute is generated. For foreign keys and Auto-increment columns no attributes will be created (for auto – increment columns refer to a later setting).
- **Create Attributes for non-empty Columns:** Using this setting, which is an enhancement of the above one defines if an Attribute is only created when a Column is not empty, which means the number of unique values in the underlying column at design time is greater than 0. Actually there is a bug in the Report Model generation engine so this setting is ignored and even if the option is checked also for empty objects and entity is built.
- **Create Attributes for auto-increment Columns:** If this option is checked the Model Generation Engine generates Attributes also for auto-increment Columns of the underlying database. This option is recommended if an auto-increment Column is also a business key in your source database and has to be contained in the generated Report Model. If this option is not checked these Columns are not taken into consideration for the generation of the Report Model. By default the Attributes generated in that way are marked as hidden in the Report Model, so if you want to make them available for your Information workers as a design element and not just as a filter-parameter you will have to do some tuning-work on the resulting Report Model later on and set the hidden property of the Attribute to false.

- **Create date variations:** If this option is checked for all found Columns of a DateTime DataType in the source database some variation - Attributes (day, month, and year) are generated and added to the resulting Report Model. Be aware that, if you want to get these variations in a localized version during the generation process you also have to run Model Designer in the desired localized version to get it correct (this is a known issue at Microsoft) otherwise the localization setting you can define later on is ignored.
- **Create numeric aggregates:** If the option is checked for each numeric Column in the source database aggregates (Sum, Avg, Min, and Max) are added to the generated Report Model. The localization of the aggregates follows the same issue as described above.
- **Create date aggregates:** If the option is checked for each DateTime Column in the source database aggregates (First, Last) are added to the Model. The localization of the aggregates follows the same issue as described above.
- **Create Roles:** If this option is checked for each relationship (foreign key) in the DSV a Role is generated in the Report Model.

Down in the lower left part of the Wizard you are requested to define the Language setting for the Report Model. Although you can change this property later it is wise to think of it in this moment, as the pluralisation of names is depending on this setting when the Report Model is generated in two passes in the next step.

The Report Model generation process uses statistics stored in the DSV file to decide how to set properties for the Entities and Attributes. The most important properties out of the big list you might see when you open the dsv file in a XML editor is:
- **Stats_RowCount:** returns the number of rows that were contained in the particular table when the DSV was created. This property affects the enumeration that chosen for the InstanceSelection Property of the report Model.

- **Stats_UniqueValuePercent:** stands for the percentage of unique values in a table and affects the type of ValueSelection and DiscourageGrouping of an Attribute as well as the generation rules for an Attribute in general.
- **Stats_MaxWidth:** defines the width of an derived Attribute

In the next step you are asked if you want to update the statistics before you generate the Report Model. Usually the statistics just have to be changed if the data source has been modified. This may happen if there is some time between the generation of the DataSource View and the Report Model itself. If you want to make sure that the Report Model is generated using the most up-to date statistics choose update statistics before generating the Report Model as this does not affect the underlying database and the amount of time Business Intelligence Studio needs to generate the Model is raised just a bit and won´t hurt in that step. The only exception is if your database has a very big number of Tables as it might end in a hang of Business Intelligence Studio, in that case its wise not to use this option. Instead, use the SQL Server Management Studio to update statistics on one table at a time or apply a T-SQL script to the database prior to the Report Model generation. If you have very large tables in your source database, you may want to update statistics on one index at a time.

As soon as you finalize the Wizard the Report Model (click on *Run*) generation starts, displays the already executed steps (and their success) and soon afterwards the raw Report Model file is available for further editing and manipulation.

If you want to generate a Report Model on an already existing (relational) DataSource on Report Server you can use Report Manager or SQL Server 2005 Management Studio, navigate to the DataSource and choose generate Report Model of the context - menu. In this scenario the needed DataSource View is automatically created behind the scenes and immediately embedded in the generated Report Model. The resulting Report Model is instantly published to the Report Server and available for your users. The only caveat is that you can`t define the rules, how the Model is generated – you have to live with the rules Microsoft uses as a standard as well as it is much more effort if you want to enhance the generated Report Model a later date.

3.2 Generating a Report Model on a multidimensional database using SQL Server Management Studio

If you want to design a Report Model on a multidimensional database like OLAP and UDM Structures (Microsoft Analysis Services 2005, there is no support for Analysis Services 2000 and SAP BW) you have to take a different approach. Assuming you have an existing multidimensional database ready and you were granted administrative rights on the database, open up Report Manager (usually http://yourserver/reports) or use SQL Server 2005 Management Studio, and click on new DataSource. Give it a name and define the connection type as Microsoft Analysis Services and type in the according connection string to your multidimensional database. Make sure you don't forget that the *Enable this DataSource* field is checked. Click on the OK button to generate the data source.

After this step you can click on the new created DataSource and are presented with a button that allows you to generate a Report Model based on the data source.

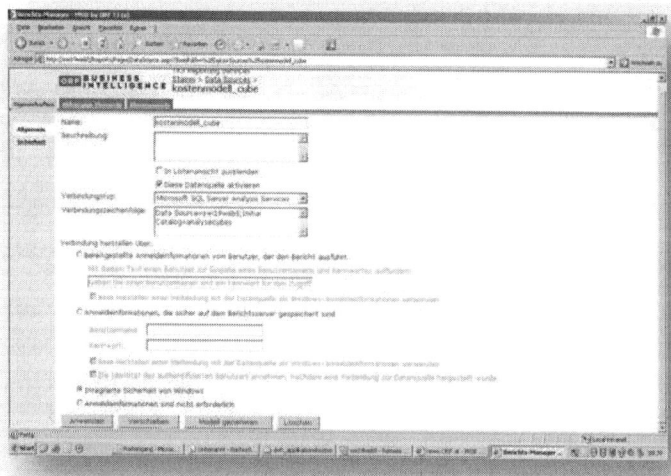

Image 5: The Model generation interface for a UDM Structure.

The Report Model is generated, using a set of internal, not changeable rules. Unfortunately right now there is no tool Microsoft provides for a further editing of such a SMDL Model generated on UDM, but they are considering a solution for non - structural changes soon. So if you want to refine the generated UDM Report Model you will have to use an XML-editor and modify the Report Model according to the information later on in this book, although Microsoft does not recommend editing these files and the possibilities to adopt some properties are very limited..

The generation of Report Models on a UDM in this version of SQL Server carries a restriction, how deep data can be explored in Report Builder. It is possible to connect a Dimension to a Measure group but not to a second related Dimension.

4 The internal structure of a Report Model

A Report Model is written in *Semantic Model Definition Language* (SMDL), which is a XML-based grammar. The namespace for SMDL is http://schemas.microsoft.com/sqlserver/*YYYY*/*MM*/semanticmodeling, where *YYYY*/*MM* indicates the date of the release of the particular version of SMDL. The SMDL Grammar is not standardised yet as Microsoft is still fine-tuning the structure and contents within the next releases of SQL Server, but there are plans to submit this grammar in the future to a standardising body. The standard file extension for SMDL files is, as you might expect it .smdl. This extension is also used by a File Sharing program named UDT (http://www.akinstaller.de) so if you use this software there is a possibility that this file extension is already associated with this software. In that case you have to keep an eye on which File you open with which application.

Be aware that all identifiers in SMDL are case-sensitive as they are based on XML and match using invariant culture.

A Report Model file is built up of three logical parts:
- **Semantic Model:** The Semantic Model contains the Business Model of the data, which is described in terms of familiar business names such as Products or Customers for the user of the Report Builder client who consumes this Report Model.
- **Physical Model:** The physical model contains, as the name implies a physical description of the source - database with optional transformations, such as defined queries within the capabilities of the Data Source View. This part of the Report Model represents the capabilities and structures of the source system that is abstracted by the model.
- **Mapping:** The mapping section finally describes how the Semantic Model is represented within the physical reality of the underlying database and binds semantic objects to their corresponding physical objects. Recapitulatory it can be said that the Mapping information is the glue that ties the physical reality and its abstraction together.

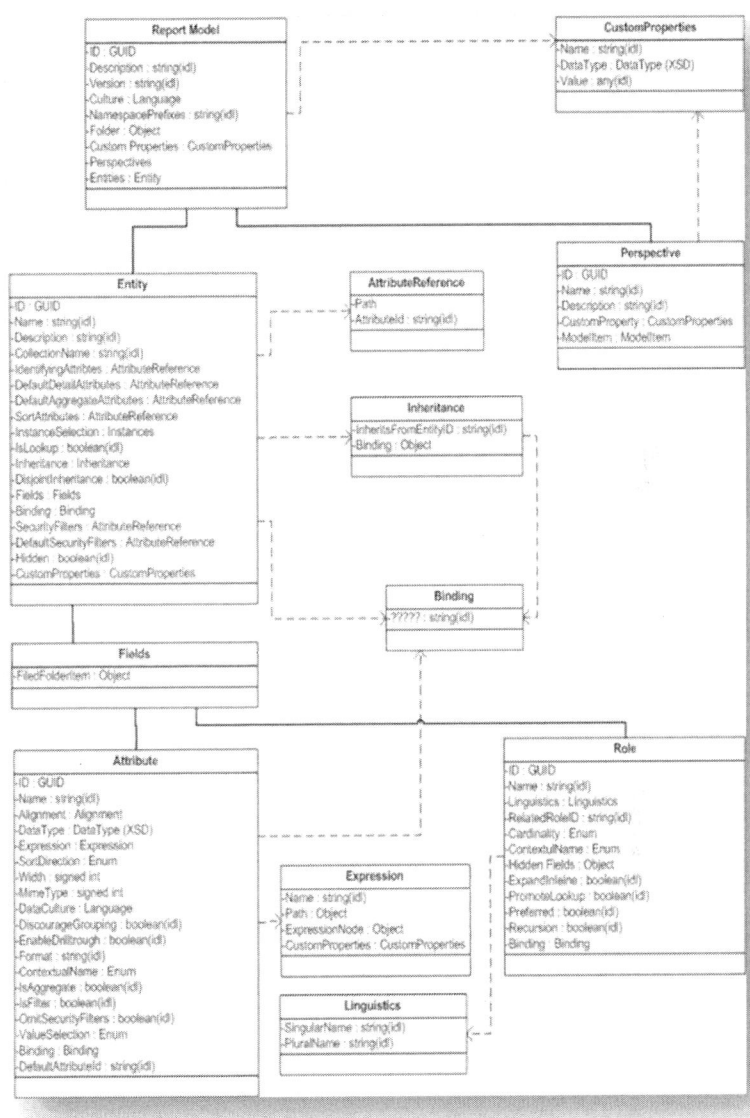

Image 6: generalised UML – Diagram of the Report Model structure

4.1 The Semantic Model object

As a first step into the internals of a Report Model and the usage - scenarios that are possible by making most out of these structures we will have a look at the root-node of the Report - Model and review its properties. As the Report Model is a XML - file you can receive a raw Report Model in an autogenerated process using Model Designer or build the file yourself. You can use appropriate Tools (e.g. XMLSpy, XML Notepad) for that task or can really dynamically generate a Report Model programmatically in a .NET application on the fly. But even if you generated the Report Model in Model Designer, you will realize that after the initial creation process it is just a raw model that needs some refinement to fit to your user's needs, so some adoptions and modifications will be required to deliver a useful and suitable solution. In the following pages I will describe the properties, their possible settings and configurations and scenarios where you might want to modify the Report Model.

4.1.1 ID

The ID – property is a GUID (Global Unique Identifier) hence an alphanumeric code that is globally unique. The ID is used internally to distinctly address any Report Model (and subsequently any element in it). The needed GUID is generated by Model Designer during the process of building the Report Model (autogenerate). It is displayed as a read-only property in Model Designer and has to keep the same value, even when the Report Model is re-generated. When writing or generating a Report Model without Microsoft's tools you have to take care that you generate and keep track of the needed GUIDs on your own.

This property has to stay absolutely fixed if you are redefining a Report Model that is published and basis for some reports already, no matter if they are published already or not. If this property is modified the existing reports will be broken and won't work either in Report Builder client or Report Manager.

4.1.2 Description:

This property is a String and is optional contained in the Report Model. The length of this String carries out of the XML-Schema no specified restriction.

Model Designer handles the job to escape the non - XML - conforming characters that may be contained in this property for you. If you enter such characters using other tools and try to open the Report Model in Model Designer or want to use it in Report Builder client, it will refuse the job with an error message, telling that the Report Model file is incorrect, so keep an eye on that when editing a Report Model outside of Microsoft´s tools.

The description will be visible for you in Report Manager in the List of objects, like the description standard Reports provide. In Report Builder client this Information is displayed in the first-steps window below the list of available Report Models, when the Information worker is required to choose a Report Model.

4.1.3 Version

The version - property is an optional contained String and accepts a free - text entry from the developer of the Report Model. This denotes that any text may be entered in that place, not just numeric version - numbers. Version - Management tools (usually) don't use this field as it is not structured in the needed way (Major.Minor.Build). As a conclusion of this fact be reminded that you have to change this number every time you change your Report Model on your own, if you want to keep the version number aligned with your builds – the version information is not automatically updated by Model Designer. As an approach for the solution later on in this book I will show an example how and where you can achieve this approach in Chapter 9.1.1.

4.1.4 Culture

The definition of culture - settings is defined as an optional language - enumeration in the SMDL - file. If you don't use Model Designer, that provides you with a list of valid language – settings when using the graphical interface to change this setting, make sure that you check the validity of your entered data according to the Microsoft - specification[5].

If no culture or an invalid culture is entered, the standard - culture of the server the Report Model resides on will be used during the runtime of the Reports based on this Report Model.

The question which culture to use first shows up as a question in the Model Generation wizard, where the developer can choose a culture. But it is also possible to change the Report Models culture later using the model´s properties, but as I mentioned earlier using the correct Culture setting when the Report Model is generated makes sure pluralisation and other initially generated information are correct and need no refinement later on.

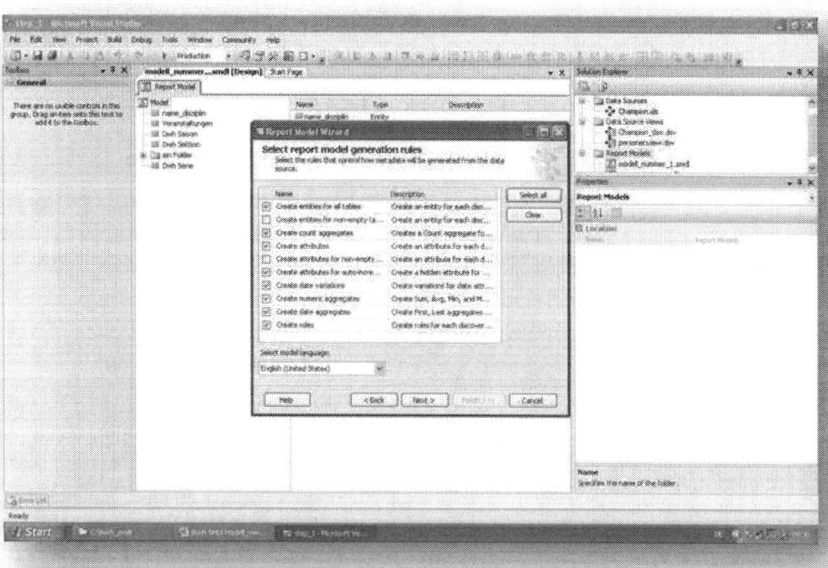

Image 7: Report Generation Wizard asking for the Culture – settings.

The defined culture – setting shows up in the way Report Builder displays a DateTime and Decimal DataType as well as

---

[5] See http://msdn2.microsoft.com/en-us/library/system.globalization.cultureinfo.aspx

the pluralisation rules for the way how collections of objects are labeled. Depending on the chosen Report Model Culture, the according way of how day, month and year are ordered is also changed.

4.1.5 DataSource View

The place where this information is stored in a Report Model differs between the local file in your development environment and the published Report Model on the Report Server.

Looking for this property in the local SMDL file won't earn a hit. The information on the DataSource View is not, as described in Books Online, contained in the Report Model file itself. Although using Model Designer, you can see a property with this name (containing a Classname - Microsoft.ReportingServices.Modeling.DataSourceView) as a value, but that's not the information you might be looking for. The information of the DataSource View is contained in another file in the same Project. Model Designer has created another SMDL Model - file behind the scene that is named like the actual project, which holds this and other project-relevant information.

De facto the majority of the information of a DataSource View is only needed during the development process in Model Designer. The DataSource View gives the developer a clipping of the whole structure of the source system, so he or she is only working on a defined subset needed. When the Report Model is built, most of the information that is contained in the DataSource View is not needed any longer as the Binding - property of entities and Attributes directly refers to the structure of the referenced database bypassing the DataSource View. The information of the DataSource View that is needed in the model, like logical keys, Named Queries which were defined there is added to the end of the Report Model during the deployment process to the targeted Report Server in this property.

4.1.6 Namespace Prefixes

In this property there are some prefixes for the contained namespaces registered. Those are needed to make up the grammar of SMDL and are automatically added by Model designer. If you create your Report Model outside the Microsoft tools you have to add these namespaces (I do recommend to uses an already generated Report Model as a blueprint) on your own. These are Namespaces for all types of Report Models:

- http://www.w3.org/2001/XMLSchema
- http://www.w3.org/2001/XMLSchema-instance
- http://schemas.microsoft.com/sqlserver/2004/10/semanticmodeling

A Report Model that is defined on a UDM structure contains some specific Namespaces to define the binding to these structures:

- http://schemas.microsoft.com/sqlserver/2004/10/semanticmodeling/udmmodeling
- http://schemas.microsoft.com/sqlserver/2004/10/semanticmodeling/udmbinding
- http://schemas.microsoft.com/sqlserver/2004/11/semanticquerydesign

4.1.7 Folder (EntityFolder)

In Model Designer the developer of the Report Model has the possibility to define folders (called EntityFolders in that place) as an additional element to arrange the Entities. The folder - property derives (inherited from the abstract type ModelItem Object) an ID, a name and a description. Optional the developer can set a Boolean switch for a hidden – property that defines if a folder is visible for the Information worker on the Report Builder client or not. If no property is set, its default value is false.

A folder may also contain custom properties and may contain entities, perspectives or other folders with no restriction on how deep they are nested. A folder is a good choice to enhance the usability of large models, containing great numbers of Entities for the Information Worker. The Report Model developer can opt to group thematic similar objects together in one folder or it is also possible to have entities show up in more folders – if that makes sense for your users. Be reminded in that step that the investigation of the wishes and demands of your users (in this place the Information

Workers who will use Report Builder client as their toolset) and the according implementation is a crucial factor for the acceptance of a Report Model in the end. Using these and other little goodies makes no or little technical difference but may enhance the usability by magnitudes.

Using a hidden Folder is also a good practice for Report Models under development that needs to be published while they are still being enhanced. You can move all the Entities that are not ready yet into this folder to make sure your Information Workers will not use them. Once an Entity is ready to be used by the Information workers just move it back from the hidden folder to the place you want it to show up.

If the Report Model is created from an UDM source, the display folders that are defined in the UDM - structure should automatically become folders in the Report Model.

The Information worker finds this EntityFolders in the Explorer – Pane of the Report Builder Client.

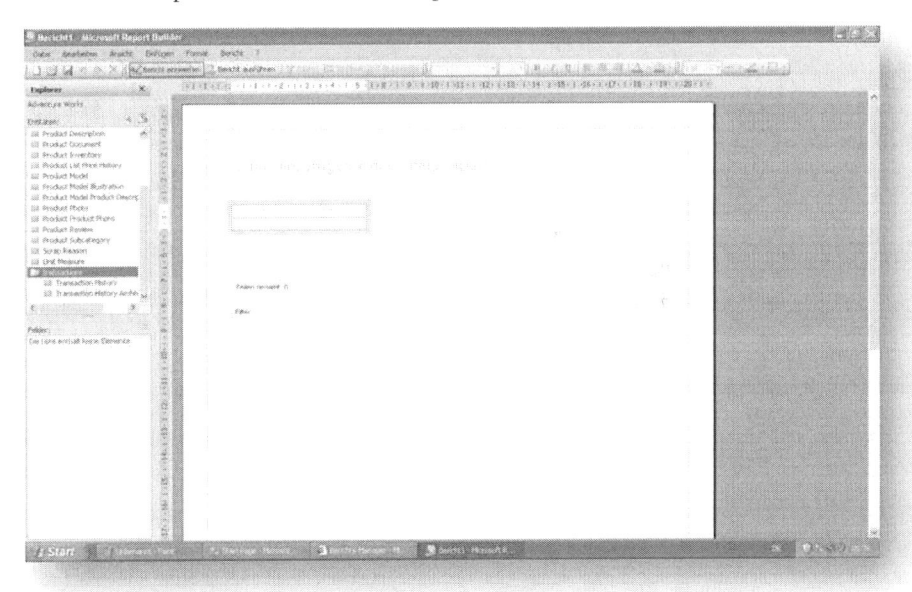

Image 8: Report Builder showing an EntityFolder

4.1.8 Custom Properties

Custom Properties are structures that allow the developer to store property – specific information in the Report Model file. This object-collection is optionally contained in a Report Model. To enter such a property a name (composed of local name and a namespace[6]), a data type (according to the XSD – Schema) and a value has to be entered.

The property names don't have to be unique.

In this release of Microsoft's tools there is no way to access this properties programmatically using the API Visual Studio uses to read/write the settings it needs. Generally spoken in this release of SQL Server it looks like the custom properties are intended to be used mainly by Microsoft's tools and not by the developers in an automated way. Maybe this approach will change in future versions. If you want to embed information in the Report Model you have to use the editor or creating tool. To embed dynamic information (for example auditing information) in the Report Model you have to write a component that manipulates the file in the process when it is been published to the Report Server like I demonstrate in Chapter 9.

4.1.9 Perspectives

Perspectives (aka as Submodels) are also a part of Report Models that hold the chance to enhance the usability for Information Workers. The developer of the Report Model has the possibility to generate perspectives in Model Designer by right clicking on the Report Model (in the Model – Tree view) and choose the command *new perspective*.

A perspective may contain entities, folders, Roles and expressions. Each perspective consists of the following properties:

- **ID** (see 0)
- **Name** (see 4.2.2) - the property has to be entered and does not allow an empty string.
- **Description** (see 0)

---

[6] The namespace is described as mandatory in the Online Documentation, but in reality it's optional.

- **Custom Property's** (see 4.1.8)
- **ModelItem:** this is a collection of Items to be included in the Submodel. In the SMDL file only the IDs of the Items are persisted, in Business Intelligence Studio these references are reverse engineered at design-time to show you the full objects and all their properties in the GUI.

The definition of perspectives is recommended if the whole Report Model would get too complex to use. This happens frequently when for example the Report Model is based on relational data of a typical OLTP system which usually contains 100 to 1000++ Tables. Another scenario would be when a usage based branching enhances the user – experience in Report Builder client. In that case you could define some perspectives and inherit the needed Entities and predefine Filters or Attributes and expressions. Also from a Security-standpoint it may be a good practice to provide different perspectives with different security-settings for different user groups. But don't be deluded in this point - obviously you can't define security – permissions on a perspective itself, but on the objects that are contained in a perspective.

Report Models that are built on a UDM structure need some special considerations. A perspective that was defined in UDM appears as a perspective with the same name in the Report Model. Items in a UDM that are not associated with a perspective will be positioned in a standard-perspective of the generated Report Model.

In Report Builder a Submodel appears for the Information worker like another data source or model he or she can choose from when designing a new Report and does not differ in his/her eyes from a *real* Report Model. The only difference is the tree-like structure as you can see in the Image below that indicates the parent Report Model of a perspective. If the Report Model is based on a UDM Structure the information worker is always presented this tree as the generation process creates at least one (default) perspective (if there are no perspectives defined in the UDM already).

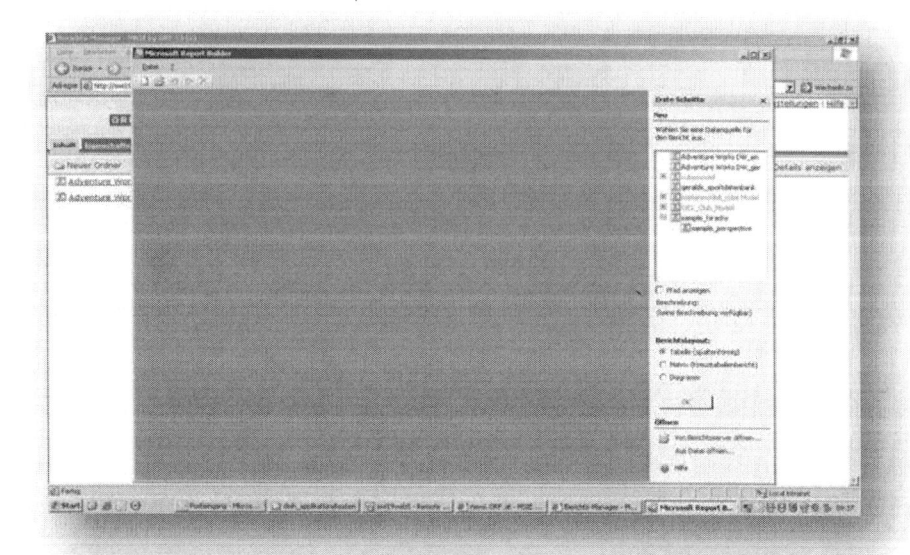

Image 9: Display of Perspectives in Report Builder

4.2 Entities

Entities are the main objects an Information Worker on the Report Builder client works with. Technically spoken they represent the according structures of the underlying Database (Tables, Views, Named Queries as well as Dimensions and Measures). For the Information workers the Entities are exposed as well known objects in their business - field with descriptive names like for example Customer, Product or Purchase.

A Table in the underlying relational database has to have a Primary Key to be used as an Entity in the Report Model. If there is no according Primary Key existing already, the developer of the Report Model has to define a Logical Primary Key in the DataSource View before the object can be used. This process also has to be taken on Views (even if they are Schema - bound) and Named Queries as they do not expose a primary key in the DSV.

If you happen to have a Table that contains a Column that is defined as a User-defined-DataType (UDT) you will get an error message[7], telling you that no Type could be found for the particular Column when trying to drag this Table into the DataSource View. The reason for that behavior is that Microsoft does not yet support User Defined DataTypes (and their capabilities) in the Business Intelligence Stack. One workaround, fitting for some scenarios where no specific output-functions of the UDT are needed, might be to use the ToString representation of the Column, defined in a Named Query or View to be the source of the data used in the DataSource View instead of the Table. The integration of UDTs into the Business Intelligence – stack is a feature Microsoft is planning for one of the next versions of SQL Server, so keep tuned if you rely on UDTs.

If the Report Model is generated from an UDM - source, Measure Groups and Dimensions will also show up as Entities in the resulting Report Model. Fact Dimensions will not result in a second Entity as the generation logic encapsulates this information in one condensed Entity.

Entities are organized in a collection of objects in the Report – Model as a child-node of the Semantic Model node (the root – node). By default (after the generation of the Report Model) the list of Entities in Model Designer as well as in Report Builder is ordered alphabetically according to the culture that was defined when generating the Report Model. But the developer of a Report Model can easily re-arrange the order in the Entities list, using the context - sensitive menu (right Mouse Button), where the option to move the Entity up/down is available. This behavior is only available in the Entities - list in the main window of Model Designer, but not in the Model – Treeview on the left side of the design surface. The re-arrangement of the entities is persisted when the SMDL – file is written to disk, so even when you regenerate your Report Model (and for example change the culture-settings) the order of the Entities will stay the same as before. The purpose of this feature is that the developer of the Report Model can make it easier usable for the Information worker, as there are business-scenarios where its wise and

---

[7] At least until SP2 of the product this behavior can be reproduced.

enhances the usability not to have an alphabetically ordered Entity List but to provide the most important Entities on top of the selection list in Report Builder client

4.2.1 ID

The ID – property is a GUID represented as an alphanumeric code that is globally unique if you are using a Report Model you generated on relational data. The ID in that case is generated by Model Designer while the Report Model is generated and is displayed as a read-only property in Model Designer. If you are compiling a Report Model on your own you also have to generate the GUIDs for the ID - property. It is important to remember that the value for the ID of an Entity has to stay unchanged even if you change substantial properties like the data-binding in Model Designer, otherwise the Reports based on this Model would be broken.

In a Report Model that is derived from an UDM Structure the situation is different. The ID in that case is not a GUID anymore; it is using an UDM Binding-Namespace to define the element in the Cube, the Entity relies on and in that way implicitly reflects the data binding properties. This textual identifier, which is based on an objects name in the UDM, is generated in the same way every time a Report Model is built so it does not break Reports based on the Report Model as long as the Names do not change in the UDM. But this statement also carries the caveat in the approach Microsoft chosed – by changing the Name of an object in the UDM all the identifiers are changed and therefore Reports built on this Report Model will be broken.

4.2.2 Name

This property defines the name an Entity is labeled in the Report Builder client. If you are using Model Designer you might encounter, that editing the name of an Entity in the properties - window is not possible as the text reverts to its original state once you leave the window or save the file. This is a known Bug prior to SP2. As a workaround you can change the name of an Entity in the Model-Tree using the rename functionality (on right mouse click) which works as expected.

In a Report Model that is generated from UDM the names show up exactly as they were defined in the cube – definition, so make sure they are named in meaningful manner as you cannot change them in that case. Microsoft does recommend that you apply a meaningful naming in the UDM Source already, but if you are unlucky enough to have to build a Report Model on a Cube you may not change you can´t edit the names in the XML-Source of the Report Model as it will break existing Reports.

4.2.3 Description

This information is of type String and is optional contained in the Report Model. It is handled in the same way as its parent description (see 0). In Report Builder client the description of an Entity is visible as a Tooltip when positioning the mouse over the particular Entity, so make sure you provide short texts as the developer of the Report Model as an extensive explanation may be unreadable in a Tooltip.

4.2.4 Collection Name

The Collection Name is an optional contained String property. It defines how a collection of those Entities should be named in the Report Builder client application (you see it for example when you have a Report based only on one Entity in the baseline of the Report). One constraint to remember on this property is that it may not be an empty string. If this property is not contained in the Report Model, the value Report Builder uses defaults to the mandatory name – property of the Entity.
During the auto generation of the Report Model the Model Designer fills this property with the name of the object the Entity is based on.

4.2.5 IdentifyingAttributes

This collection of object - properties has to contain at least one entry. It contains references to all Attributes that (logically) allow distinctly identify an instance of the Entity.
The collection contains Attribute - references using their IDs (remember – their structure is different in relational Models and UDM Models). Additionally, an optional name and a path may be entered as properties. While the path property is read

– only in Business Intelligence Studio and can't be used in this situation the name - property can be edited. In the Report Model file the name is not natively contained in the XML - schema. But to make the Report Model easier human - readable Microsoft chosed to add a XML – comment - line with the name above each Attribute - reference entry. This information is not used in Business Intelligence Studio to display this information. If you remove one of these lines the name - property is still well filled – it is dynamically retrieved when needed by Business Intelligence Studio using the ID of the Attribute.

During the automatic generation of the Report Model Business Intelligence Studio applies the Primary Key of the underlying Table as a best guess for the value. The auto generation process avoids using numbers as IdentifyingAttributes and has an internal Score-logic to determine the best suited Attributes for this collection. If your scenario builds on numeric Attributes, like Part Numbers or Invoice Numbers you will have to modify the generated Report Model to fit to your needs.

Report Builder uses the IdentifyingAttributes for instance selection where the Information worker or end-user is presented a concatenated Value of all the chosen Attributes to choose from.

Be aware that, if the chosen Attributes are not unique identifying an instance of the Entity, your Information workers might not get the data out of the system they should get.

4.2.6 DefaultDetailAttributes

The collection of DefaultDetailAttributes defines which Attributes are automatically shown when a user of the Report Builder client drags the whole Entity on the Design Surface. A second occurrence are the generated Click Trough Reports for an Entity, they also display the collection of DefaultDetail Attributes. In this release of Report Builder there is no way to distinguish the properties for the two purposes so each Item you choose for Click Trough also applies for the design time experience in Report Builder client. So it is your job as the developer of the Report Model to choose wisely which

Attributes are contained in this collection. This collection is optional in the Report Model, so it may contain between 0 and n Attribute - references. The objects structure is an Attribute – Reference analogues as the one I described in chapter 4.2.5.

The Report Model generation engine uses an internal score-logic on the underlying schema and data to decide which the best suited Attributes are, that this collection is populated with during the generation process.

You should review this collection to contain the most needed and identifying Attributes of this Entity according to the expected usage scenarios.

4.2.7 DefaultAggregate Attributes

This collection that has to contain at least one entry that defines the Attributes that are used in an aggregation from a different Entity to drill down to that Entity (on a one-to-many-relationship). The defined Attributes are displayed in Report Builder client when this Entity is acting as an aggregate. Although you are free to select every Attribute in Model Designer you are just allowed to add aggregatable Attributes to this collection. An aggregate able Attribute is defined as an Attribute that has at least one aggregating function (like count) contained in an expression defining the Attribute. Trying to add a standard Attribute without an aggregation function to this collection earns you an Error Message when you try to build or deploy the Report Model. As every Attribute that is contained in this collection is used for grouping purposes choose wisely how many items you want to use in this place as too many of them might confuse your Information workers.

The structure of the Attribute references apply to the same rules as described in 4.2.5

In ad hoc Reports these Attributes (belonging to another Entity) are shown in the generated Click Trough Reports when the other entities have a one-to-many-relationship to this Entity.

4.2.8 Sort Attributes

The sort Attributes collection is a list of references to Attributes that are used to specify the default sort order of the whole Entity if there is no user defined sorting selected in Report Builder client. Compared to the other used Attributes collections in that case the collection not only contains Attribute References, but may also include a SortDirection property as an own XML-Node to define weather the sorting happens ascending or descending. If the Property is not set or existing in the Report Model its default value is ascending.

If the Report Model is based on an UDM structure be informed that the sort order that was defined in the Cube – definition, especially user defined sorting and date-sorting, cannot be transferred into the generated Report Model and get lost.

4.2.9 InstanceSelection

This property is defined as an enumeration and sets how a user on the Report Builder client can select an instance out of this Entity (for example when filtering or building an expression). The displayed name is the concatenation of the defined IdentifyingAttributes of the Entity. In the Autogenerate Process Model Designer tries to make a best – guess based on the Table statistics of the underlying database (Stats_RowCount in the DataSource View) to determine which values to use.

But as a Report Model is often generated quite early in the lifecycle of a database project it makes sense to consider reviewing this property some time after the Report Model is generated and the database carries a real world-load. At the point in time when the Report Model is generated, the Database may contain only a little amount data, so probably all InstanceSelections are set to dropdown, but later when the database is used and the amount of data grows this option is no longer the best for the information worker. So I do recommend that you review and modify this property according to the amount of data you prognose for each Entity:

- **Dropdown:** When the number of instances in the underlying data source is small enough to fit in a dropdown list, which is up to 200 entries, this option is chosen by the Report Model generation engine.

- **List:** This option should be used if the number of instances is too big for a dropdown but still needs no pre-filtering. If the table the Entity is based on contains between 200 and 500 entries this option is suggested by the generation engine.
- **FilteredList:** This option enhances the basic List described already and should be used if the number of instances will be that large that a filtering by the information worker or end-user is needed (or recommended) prior to displaying a list of values. The engine that creates a Report Model chooses this approach if the table it is based on contains between 500 and 5000 entries.
- **MandatoryFilter:** The functionality of this List is like the FilteredList but with one difference – in this case, due to the very big number of instances that may be contained in the Entity it is mandatory for the Information worker or end-user to filter the values before he or she can make a selection. This option is preferred for Entities that contain more than 5000 instances

If the Model is based on a UDM Model that Attribute is derived from the InstanceSelection property of an entity there.

4.2.10 IsLookup

This Boolean property defines if the according Entity is handled as a fully fledged Entity in the Report Builder application or if it only acts as a Lookup. The property is optional contained in the Report Model; if it is not set it defaults to false.

Books Online states that only one IdentifyingAttribute is allowed in an Entity to be defined as a lookup, but in reality it also works out with more Identifying Attributes. Although the developer just sees the first Identifying Attribute in the parent Entity in the Model Designer environment the Information worker receives all Identifying Attributes in Report Builder client. The only caveat is that for the additional Attributes the naming – model can´t be defined in Business Intelligence Studio. Reporting Services automatically uses the Merge – option for those Attributes.

If an Entity is defined as a Lookup Entity it is not visible in the Entity's – list for the Information worker. The Identifying Attributes of the Lookup – Entity are displayed in its parent Entity as if they were native attributes of the parent Entity. The Lookup - Entities are only visible if the Information worker is defining Filters in Report Builder to be used as a filtering condition. The usage of Lookup - Entities is recommended if the developer wants to denormalize hierarchical structures or just simplify the Report Model (for example if the information of some Entities is simply to less to display them as an own object for the Information worker). Assume you have a Table Country's and a Table with Regions in the Countries in your Database. If you autogenerate the Model you earn two separated Entities. But if the Information worker or end user demands a list where he or she can choose a Region and the Country it is contained in this Entity, you will have to use this feature.

In the sample aw_lookup I did that for the *ProductDocuments* and *Documents* Entity. Having a look on the Data Model you will see that the *Products* Table has a logical connection to the *Documents* Table, but in between is the *ProductDocuments* Table. One way to overcome this dilemma is to define the *Documents* Table as a Lookup to the *ProductDocuments* Entity. Doing this you get the IdentifyingAttributes of the *Documents* Table (the File Name in this case) mirrored into the *ProductDocuments* Entity when using it in Report Builder client (and you also might realize that a new type of Role is added to the Entities referencing the fresh defined Lookup). The contents of the Lookup Entity are ordered in the Attributes list in the place it (respective the Role connecting to Entity) was positioned when being defined as a Lookup Entity.

An Entity that only contains one Attribute that has its hidden – property set to true will be defined as a Lookup-Entity during the Model generation by the Report Model generation engine.

If you define a multi-level hierarchy flattened using a lookup-structure make sure you don't forget to set the *PromoteLookup*

Flag of the connecting Roles to true, so the lookup-information is mirrored trough the different levels. I showcased this also in the aw_lookup sample using the Product hierarchy. The Product has a Relationship to the *ProductSubcategory* Table and this one has a relationship to the *ProductCategory* Table. The task I wanted to fulfill is to have the *ProductCategory* and the *ProductSubcategory* available in the *Products* Entity. To achieve to solution I did the following steps:

- Define the ProductCategory Entity as a Lookup and making sure the Category name is set as an Identifying attribute.
- Define the ProductSubcategory as a Lookup and making sure the Category name is set as an Identifying attribute (I changed the names of the Attributes so they don't mess up in the Report I will generate later on).
- Setting the PromoteLookup property of the Role that is connecting Category to Subcategory to true

When designing a Report on this Model you will see the ProductSubcategory Attribute in the Product Entity. If you drag this Attribute to the Design Surface, you will also get the ProductCategory included which is retrieved as a promoted lookup.

4.2.11 Inheritence

Defines how an Entity inherits Roles, Attributes and Expressions from another (referred to as its parent) Entity. The object is defined as an InheritsFromEntityID, which defines the Entity that is the parent and a type of binding. Keep in mind that it is not possible that the Entity an inheritance is defined on may not be contained the inheritance – chain (so no self-Inheritence is possible).

One common scenario for the use of inheritance would be a denormalization-scenario where one Entity is a kind of the other. So if there is a general Entity Product that holds all the Standard-Attributes (weight, sizes, etc…) and there are some Entities for special Products, your Information worker or end-user wants to see all Attributes. In that case an Inheritance is recommended.

As a sample have a look on the aw_inheritence Report Model where I modeled the same case as in the aw_lookup sample. There is a logical connection between *Documents* (the document itself, its properties) to the *Product*. But unfortunately in the relational Data Model (visible in the DSV) there is an intermediate Table between those two. So the Solution in this place was to define an Inheritance on this intermediate table so it inherits **all** of the documents tables Attributes and Roles, opposed to the IsLookup parameter that only delivers the identifying attributes of the referenced Entity.

An Inheritance is defined as you enter the ID of the parent's Entity; the actual Entity should inherit its additional properties from. In the underlying DSV there has to be a foreign key defined that you also have to provide to define the Inheritance, otherwise the build process will fail. The reason is that the merged display in Report Builder is just a UI-trick, so behind the scenes the join-definition is needed to retrieve the data. Be aware that Model Designer creates a Role in the autogenerate process to reflect this structure, so don't forget to delete or hide this Role if you define an Inheritence.

When an Entity has direct ancestors and/or descendents (using inheritance), all Fields and Roles from the ancestors and descendents of the current Entity are displayed in the Explorer pane and the Fields List of the Report Builder as if they belonged to the current Entity itself.

Items are displayed in the following order:
1. from the inheritance root
2. all direct ancestors in order
3. the current Entity
4. then all direct descendents in an undefined order
   Report Builder only shows the direct Inheritence (ancestors, descents) by default. Other relationships (aunts, uncles, etc) are only displayed in the Advanced Explorer Mode.

4.2.12 Disjoint Inheritence

This Boolean property, when set to true, displays Entities that inherit from this Entity as mutually exclusive sets. This property has to be defined by the Model Designer to make sure Objects that relate to the same parent are not mixed (based on knowledge of the contained data). The default value of this optional property is false.

4.2.13 Fields

The (calculated) Fields are a Collection as child of the Entity. They are described in detail in Chapter 9.1.2

4.2.14 Binding

The Binding – Property that is mandatory and of type object defines the object in the Data Source View (resp. the underlying DataSource) the Entity is based on. This information is needed on the Report Builder/Report Server side to translate the Semantic Queries that are defined against the Report Model into SQL or MDX Statements.

If you open a SMDL file you won´t find such a property. But there is another property, which is not described in the Books online that fulfills the described duties. Its property name is Table and it has a Name - Attribute that contains the text of the underlying objects name in the DataSource View. When the Report Model is published to the Report Server this property changes and the Binding - information and the information contained in the DataSource View are merged together.

In a Report Model that is based on a UDM, the binding is handled in a different way, using custom properties for this task. The following set of properties is used to define the binding:

- DbDimensionBinding: String
- DbUniqueDimensionBinding: String
- EntityOrigin: String
- DimensionType: short

4.2.15 SecurityFilter

This optional property - collection defines the filters (expressions) that act as a security filter. If no security filter is defined, every user who uses the Report Model gets all data that is contained in the Entity. But once a security filter is set, a query that is started on the Report Builder client or the generated Reports that reference the Entity gets all of these filters that are contained in this collection added to the query. A person only sees the data where those filters to which he has permission to apply. Each Filter that is defined is a securable element where the developer or administrator can set permissions (see chapter 7) on.

Although you can enter any attribute into that collection in Business Intelligence Studio, it is only allowed to add real Filters into this collection. Otherwise you will get an Error if you try to compile or deploy the Report Model. How to define (named) Filters is described in Chapter 4.6.

If security filters are defined and none of them are available for an end-user, all instances of the Entity are filtered out – so no data is retrieved. For entities with inheritance, the security filters for all ancestor entities are applied as well.

To give you an impression how to use this functionality here is a small textual example:

- There is a Table in the database that contains sales - data for a product divided up by regions. So in a region - Column of the Table there is defined if the sale took place in North, South or Central region.
- In Model Designer the developer can define a set of filters. For example a Filter_north where an expression like Region='North' is defined as filter-condition (for the simplicity of the sample I am not referring to personalized filters that depend on the ID of the particular user in this chapter).
- In the next step the developer adds all these filters to the SecurityFilters collection of the sales Entity in Model Designer.
- The administrator or developer of the report Server the Report Mode has been published on afterwards

has the possibility to assign security permissions to these filters in Management Studio. So Sue (the North-Agent) gets permission for the North Filter, John (who is responsible for South and central) gets permission for the Central and South filter. The Boss gets Permissions for all Filters and Doe who is an internal got no permissions assigned. Again for the simplicity of the Sample I do not refer to Groups (Active directory) or references in the database (the Sales agents and their Territories could also be defined in the database)
- When these persons are consuming a Report generated on this Report Model Sue will just get sales from the North region, John gets sales from Central and South and the Boss sees every sale. Doe will not see a simple row of data if he opens the same Report.

4.2.16 Default Security Filter

This optional property collection defines a set of standard security filters that are applied when no Security Filters for a user are available (for example when the user does not have the sufficient permissions). As described earlier, when no security filter is put on an Entity the information worker and end-user can access all data without restrictions. But if there is one Security Filter set, and the particular user does not have permissions for this filter, he or she would see nothing (like Doe in our previous sample). If that is not the intended behavior, the developer can define a filter, which is used by the Reporting Engine when none of the defined Security Filters apply. For more information on Security concepts in Report Builder see Chapter 7.1

4.2.17 Hidden

This optional property defines weather the Information worker can see this Entity in Report Builder or not. The property is optional; if it is not set it defaults to false.
If you have Entities in the Model that Business Intelligence Studio generated, that you don't need in the Model any more it proofed as a better way to set the hidden Property to true

than to delete them, especially if the Report Model has been out in the wild already and you don't want to break existing Reports built on that Report Model. If for any reason you have to update the Report Model (using the auto generate feature) the deleted items are created again, whereas the hidden property will not be touched.

4.2.18 Custom Properties

See Chapter 4.1.8

4.3 Fields

Fields are defined as an abstract type within an Entity. It can either be an Attribute, a Filter or a Role. All of these types inherit their base structure from the ModelItem and are displayed together in the Fields list in the Model designer. Similar to the Entities the Model Developer can modify the display - order of the items, but just keep in mind that Attributes, Roles and filters are ordered in one list.

4.4 Attributes

An Attribute is a detailed piece of information contained within an Entity. Attributes are the details that describe a particular instance of an Entity. Attributes are a logical representation of the Tables or View's Columns of the underlying DataSource. Depending on the rules that are used to generate the Report Model Auto Increment Columns of the underlying database are hidden or omitted. Numeric Columns are enhanced with a set of aggregates (Total, Avg, Min, Max) and DateTime Columns earn some fraction – Attributes (day, month, year) as well as some aggregates (first, last).

If the Report Model is generated from an UDM source the Measures and Dimension - Attributes of this structure also will be represented as Attributes. Calculated Members of a Unified Dimensional Model will also turn into an Attribute during the Model generation process. Key Performance Indicators (KPIs) are represented as a set of Attributes in the Report Model. For each functionality of a KPI (Goal, Value, Status, Trend) you will find one Attribute, also the graphics are represented as own (binary) Attributes. But be aware that only KPIs and calculations that are associated with a Measure Group will be considered in

the generation of the Report Model, all others are omitted. Keep in mind that right now Report Models do not have the concept of hierarchies, which means that parent-child hierarchies can't be transferred into the Report Model in this version of SQL Server.
The actions of a cube are also not transferred into the Report Model. It is a good practice to establish a data dictionary to have a place where UDM specific information that is not transferable into a Report Model can be stored and made accessible for the information worker.

4.4.1 ID

See chapter 4.1.1

4.4.2 Name

This property is a String and defines how an Attribute can be identified by the information worker in Report Builder client. The property is mandatory if the Attribute is directly derived from a source - Column and does not have an expression. Although the documentation indicates that the name is only mandatory in case of a non - expression attribute, Model Designer does not allow you to build a Report Model with an empty Name – String, even the Attribute is based on an expression.

During the autogenerate process Attribute names are generated using existing capital letters in the Column name of the source object as a spacing indicator. So for example the Column *CustomerName* will be named *Customer Name* as Attribute in the Report Model. If the Table name is contained in the Column name, which is a common practice for OLTP Systems, you will either have to modify the Names in the DataSource View or edit this property to strip the name down.

In Model Designer the handling of the name – property for an Attribute shows the same Bug as in 4.2.2.

In a Report Model that is generated from UDM the names show up exactly as they were defined in the cube – definition, so make sure they are named in meaningful manner as you cannot change them without braking the Report Model.

4.4.3 Description

This information is of type String and is optional contained in the Report Model. It is handled in the same way as its parent description (see 4.1.2). If your Report Model is based on a relational SQL Server Database, you might assume that the Description that may be entered in the Column Definition will be found in that place, but that is not the case. The Description - Information of the source system is not contained in the DataSource View and therefore also not available in the generated Report Model.

The description renders itself as a Tooltip in Report Builder when the Information worker is hovering the mouse over the Attributes – list like it does with the Entities. In this place also the recommendation applies to keep the description short, an extensive Tooltip is hard to read for your Information workers

4.4.4 Alignment

The alignment property defines the default alignment of the Attribute in a table or matrix layout when it is dropped on the Design Surface of the Report Builder client. Valid members of this enumeration are left, right, center and general (general means that Text and Boolean Data is aligned to the left, numeric and DateTime data is aligned to the right) which need no further description. If no alignment is defined the general – value is used.

4.4.5 DataType

The Datatypes of Columns of the underlying Database are mapped to the Report Models Types. This mapping is not done directly from Database types to Report Model types; the connecting piece in this place is the CLR-Type that has a direct mapping into a Report Model type. This property that is an enumeration that contains these values:

- **Boolean**
- **DateTime**
- **Integer:** This DataType contains the Int16, Int32, Uint16, Byte and SByte CLR Types.
- **Decimal:** This DataType acts as a pool for the Decimal, Int64, UInt32 and UInt64 CLR Types.

- **Float** summarizes the Single and Double CLR Type.
- **String** represents all data contained in String, Char and the GUID CLR Type
- **Binary** is a representation of the Byte [] (Byte array) CLR Type.
- **EntityKey:** This DataType is not mapped to any specific CLR Type. It is a base-64 encoded binary value that uniquely describes an instance of an Entity. An EntityKey is created as a composite of the Key Columns (Primary key, Foreign Keys) for the Entity. The first byte is reserved for internal use and must equal zero. The trailing bytes represent a binary serialization of the key Columns in the Table to which the Entity or Column is bound in their native types. Key Columns are serialized in the order in which they are defined in the primary key list in the physical model. The EntityKey is a DataType the Semantic Query Engine uses to get some performance gains in the creation of aggregations like COUNT.

One of the values has to be provided in the Report Model and defines the Attribute's data type in Report Builder. If the Attribute is based on an Expression both types (output of the Expression and Attribute) have to match. If the Attribute is not based on an Expression, the selected DataType has to match to the DataType of the underlying Column, as the following matrix for SQL Server 2005 shows; otherwise Model Designer will refuse to build and deploy it with an error. The DataType is represented graphically in Model Designer as well as in Report Builder client. A change of this property in Model Designer does not refresh the GUI, also the refresh button does not work in here, it is only reflected after you close the Model and then reopen it again.

The Datatypes of SQL Server 2005 (relational Engine) map to the Report Models Datatypes as described in the following Table:

	Boolean	DateTime	Integer	Decimal	Float	String	Binary
Bigint				x			
Binary							x
Bit	x						
Char						x	
DateTime		x					
Decimal				x			
Float					x		
Image							x
int			x				
money				x			
Nchar						x	
Ntext						x	
numeric				x			
nvarchar						x	
nvarchar(max)						x	
Real					x		
smalldatetime		x					
smallint			x				
smallmoney				x			
sql_variant	None – needs to be converted in the DSV in a named query
Text						x	
timestamp							x
tinyint			x				
uniqueidentifyer						x	
varbinary							
varbinary(max)							
varchar						x	

varchar(max)						x	
XML						x	

The Oracle – Datatypes map as follows:

	Boolean	DateTime	Integer	Decimal	Float	String	Binary
BFILE							x
BLOB							x
CHAR						x	
CLOB						X	
DATE		X					
FLOAT				x			
INTEGER			x				
INTERVAL YEAR TO MONTH			x				
INTERVAL DAY TO SECOND		X					
LONG						x	
LONG RAW							x
NCHAR						x	
NCLOB						x	
NUMBER				x			
NVARCHAR2						x	
RAW							X
ROWID						X	
TIMESTAMP		X					
TIMESTAMP WITH LOCAL TIME ZONE		X					
TIMESTAMP WITH TIME ZONE		X					

UNSIGNED INTEGER		X			
VARCHAR2					X

4.4.6 Nullable

The Boolean property defines if an Attribute can have NULL – values or not. This property is derived from the underlying Column - definition, and must match if the Attribute is directly based on a Column. If the Attribute is based on an Expression, the developer has to define weather the Attribute may contain NULL – values or not. This property is optional and defaults false when it is not contained in the Report Model. One common problem you may run into is that the Nullability of an Attribute is derived from the underlying table. If, for some reasons you have to replace this Table in the DSV with a named query all Objects will need to be defined as Nullable (in a Query no column can be defined as not-nullable) otherwise the Report Model cannot be built.

4.4.7 Expression

An Expression is an object that defines how a derived Attribute is defined. To be valid a scalar value, according to one of the possible data types has to be returned by the formula. An Expression is represented in a nested way in the SMDL File. In the expression- node there is a function-node that defines the one or more functions that make up the whole expression. As a sibling the attributes with their references (IDs) are defined. If you enter a more complex expression you will see that the storage mechanism in the file can get quite confusing. How to deal with expressions in general is described in chapter 4.7

4.4.8 SortDirection

The default SortDirection of an Attribute is defined in this property. This information is used if there is no user defined sorting chosen in the generated ad hoc Reports. It allows an enumeration that contains ascending, descending and none as valid values. The default value is ascending.
If your Report Model is based on Analysis Services the Sort order defined in this place will not be preserved, especially

time – Attributes and user defined sorting cannot be transferred into the Report Model.

4.4.9 Width

The width defines how many characters a Column measures as default in Report Builder client when the Attribute is dropped on the Design Surface. The default value of this optional integer value depends on the defined data type of the Attribute:

- Boolean   6
- DateTime   10
- Integer   8
- Decimal   8
- Float   8
- String   20
- Binary   1023
- EntityKey   128

But keep in mind that in Report Builder client also the name of an Attribute is used to define the optimal width the Column gets. The broader value of Name and Width defines the actual sizing.

4.4.10 MimeType

This property is only used if the Attribute is defined as a binary DataType, for the other Datatypes it is ignored. This string may not be empty in the case of a binary Attribute and describes the Content-Type that is contained in the binary stream, to correctly represent it in Report Builder. In this version of Report Models only Image-Types according to the following Mime-types are allowed:

- image\bmp
- image\jpeg
- image\x-png
- image\png
- image\gif

For all Datatypes of the relational Database during Model – generation the MimeType is set to image/jpeg. If you have a column in your database that carries different types of images (one row contains a jpeg, one row a png, ..) you will have to apply some logic on the DSV-Side to split the information up into more columns (one jpeg column, one png column) based on the provided metadata and set the according Mime Type as one Attribute can only be of one MimeType.

4.4.11 DataCulture

This property indicates the culture to be used for culture-sensitive operations, for example how numerical data (out of an Expression) is formatted with a currency symbol. This culture is not used for simple display formatting, such as for date or numeric formats. If not specified, the DataCulture defaults to the Report Model Culture, if you want to supply a setting it has to be in the allowed cultures enumeration, which can be reviewed under http://msdn2.microsoft.com/en-us/library/system.globalization.cultureinfo.aspx

4.4.12 DiscourageGrouping

This optional Boolean property prohibits the Report Builder client, when set to true, that this Attribute is used for grouping purposes. This property is to be used when an Attribute is highly unique in the business context, so that grouping by it does not make sense. The Model generation engine sets this property to true if the uniqueness of an attribute in the underlying DataSource exceeds the value of 80 percent.
If the Report Model is based on a UDM this property is derived from the GroupingBehaviour settings of the UDM.

4.4.13 EnableDrilltrough

This Boolean optional property defines if the end-user, who consumes the Report, is allowed to Clickthrough on this Attribute to access the base Entity. The property is optional and if it is not contained in the model it defaults to false. For more information about Clickthrough Reports, the limitations and the Report Model settings you have to take into account I refer to chapter 6.10

4.4.14 Format

To define an output format Report Model allows the default .Net format strings (see http://msdn2.microsoft.com/en-us/library/fbxft59x.aspx) to be used to define the format the value of the Attribute in Report Builder client.

Besides these standard .Net formats, the following additional format strings are supported in Report Models:

Format Strings for DateTime
- ddd: day of week abbreviation
- dddd: full day of week name
- MMM: month abbreviation
- MMMM:full month name

Format Strings for Booleans
- True/false: "True" and "False"
- Yes/no: "Yes" and "No"

4.4.15 ContextualName

This property defines how Report Builder should generate a context-sensitive name for this Attribute when the containing Entity is reached using a Role. The enumerator can be one of three values:

- **Attribute:** the name of the Attribute itself is used as the contextual name.
- **Merge:** the name of the Attribute and the name of the particular Role used to reach the Attribute are merged together as the contextual name.
- **Role:** If the particular Attribute is the only identifying Attribute of the Entity, this enumeration uses the Role name as the contextual name. If the Attribute is not the identifying Attribute of the Entity the enumeration is treated like merge.

The enumerator value defaults to Attribute.

4.4.16 IsAggregate

This optional Boolean property indicates whether the Attribute is one on which an aggregate can be calculated not just in the context of the containing Entity, but also for any other Entity for which is connected in an one - to - many relationship. Practically the description means that if set to true this Attribute can be used for the calculation of totals and subtotals in a Report Builder Report. If this property is not set or defined it defaults to false, so the Attribute is treated as a scalar, non aggregatable value. This property is useful to define numerical values which usually would be treated aggregatable (for example part-numbers, account-numbers, etc) that may not be aggregated.

IsAggregate can only be true for Attributes with non-anchored expressions.

4.4.17 IsFilter

This optional Boolean property defines weather the affected Attribute can be used as a named Filter in Report Builder client or not. It can only be true for Boolean Attributes if defined as a native Attribute, otherwise the Report Model can't be built. The default value of this property is false. The proper use of this feature is to define a filter with a Name in an Entity. The Information worker in Report Builder can use this named filter as a filter - criteria that only return true or false. In that way the developer of the Report Model can design and provide named filters that probably would be too complex to build for the Information worker and make them available for him or her without requiring or allowing insight into the way the filter is set up.

4.4.18 OmitSecurityFilters

This property indicates that the expression, used for the calculation of this Attribute should be handled without adding security filters. This setting is typically used for cases where detail data must be secured based on security filters but the aggregate data is public. This Boolean property is ignored when the Attribute does not have an expression.

4.4.19 ValueSelection

This property determines the behaviour of Report Builder client for the selection of values of the particular Attribute, based on the expected number of unique values in the underlying database.

Three options of the enumeration are available:

- **None:** This setting requires the Information worker in the Report Builder client to explicitly type in a value. This option is good for any number of expected instances, but is of course the least user – friendly one as the Users have to know for which particular value they are searching without any hint for the existing data from the system.
- **Dropdown:** If this setting is chosen, the unique values of this Attribute are displayed in a simple dropdown list. This option works well for up to 200 instances.
- **List.** Using that setting displays the unique values in a list to select from. That approach is chosen by the Report Model generation engine if there are between 200 and 1000 instances.

Keep in mind, that if the IsAggregate property of this Attribute is set to True, this setting is ignored.

If the Model is based on a UDM Model this Attribute is derived from the InstanceSelection property there.

4.4.20 Binding

The binding – property defines on which Column in the Data Source View the Attribute is bound. The details on this property can be found in 4.2.14. Likewise in the referenced chapter also for Attributes the binding is slightly different then described in Books Online.

In a Model based on relational data, there is a Column - node that has a name-Attribute, which defines the Column in the DataSourceView the Attribute, is based on.

A Model that is generated on a UDM Structure defines its Binding in the following custom properties:

- AttributeBinding
- UniqueAttributeBinding
- AttributeOrigin
- AllMemberBinding

4.4.21 Default Aggregate Attribute

The property defines the Identifier of the Attribute which should act as the default aggregate for this Attribute. Note that this string must be the ID of a Variation of this Attribute. This string is not allowed if the IsAggregate property is specified as True. The value is ignored if the Attribute is hidden.

4.5 Roles

A Role is the description of the logical relationship between two Entities. For the technical user this object refers to a foreign key constraint of a relational database or the Fact - Dimension relations in a UDM, but for the business user and the Information worker it simply defines the interactions between two Entities.

Recursive Roles in the underlying DataSource generate two Roles in the Report Model (one for each direction) as the Roles in a Report Model are always treated in a monodirectional way.

In a Report Model that was built on a UDM there is a limitation on which data can be reached.

4.5.1 ID

See 4.1.1

4.5.2 Name

This mandatory property defines the name of the Role as it is visible in Report Builder client as an optional string. If the cardinality of the Role is One or OptionalOne, the name of the so related Entity is the default value of the Role if you don't provide one. Otherwise, the string value defaults to the CollectionName of the related Entity.

4.5.3 Description

This information is of type String and is optional contained in the Report Model. It is handled in the same way as its parent description (see 4.1.2).

The description renders itself as Tooltip in Report Builder client when the Information worker is moving the mouse over the Attributes – list like it does with the Entities. So also keep an eye on the length and readability of the text you enter.

4.5.4 Linguistics

The Linguistics property of the Role is optional contained in the Report Model. The singular and plural names of the

Entities that are connected by this Role are built for display in Report Builder client depending on the cardinality of the relationship and this information. When the Information worker is navigating from one to many, the plural name is used; when going from one to one, the singular name is used. This property is not allowed if the name of the Role is not defined. In this case, SingularName and PluralName default to the name of the related Entity.

4.5.5 RelatedRoleID

This property defines the ID of the corresponding Role (that navigates vice-versa) on the target Entity. In short the definition is as follows:

- You have an Entity *a* and an Entity *b*
- You define a Role *x* that navigates you from *a* to *b*
- The Related Role of x is the particular Role that navigates back from b to a

With that definition it is obvious that the RelatedRole cannot be the same as the Role containing it. Usually you will not have the demand to change these settings, only in rare Cases where the transverse way of a role has to take another path as the one defined in the data model of the source system for logical or business reasons.

4.5.6 Cardinality

The mandatory parameter is built of an enumeration of the following Members, which define how the connection between the two partners of the Role is set up. During the build - process of a Report Model the engine decides the best guess for this option by taking the foreign key constraints and the (unique) indexes into account.

- **One:** The one participant of the Role has exactly one corresponding partner.
- **Many:** The one participant of the Role has one ore many corresponding partners.
- **OptionalOne:** The one participant of the Role has no or exactly one corresponding partner.
- **OptionalMany:** The one participant of the Role has no or many corresponding partners.

You may miss one option in this collection – there is no direct support for a many-to-many relationship (m:n) in the definition of a Role. As there is usually a third partner (Intersection Table) involved in this scenario it is not just done using an option in the cardinality. In Chapter 9.1.3 I will describe what is needed to correctly display and use such a relationship in Report Builder client.

If you modify this setting in Model Designer the Report Model compiles, no matter how you change the cardinality and it is representing the source system´s reality or not. But you might get a warning.

Another special case of a Cardinality is the Primary Address Problem that deals with the convenient display of a multiple relationship between two entities which is described in Chapter 9.1.4

4.5.7 ContextualName

When the particular Role is used to reach a specific Entity in Report Builder, the ContextualName enumerator of the Role overrides the ContextualName setting for Attributes in the Role's target Entity.

The enumerator contains three values:
- **Attribute:** The name of the Attribute that is reached by this Role is used as the ContextualName.
- **Merge:** If this option is used the name of the Attribute and the Role are concatenated and used as the ContextualName.
- **Role:** If the Attribute targeted with this Role is the single identifying Attribute of the Entity, specifying Role uses the Role name as the contextual name. If it is not the single identifying Attribute of the Entity, Role is treated like Merge.

The enumerator value defaults to Attribute.

4.5.8 HiddenFields

This property defines a set of fields (Attributes and Roles) and/or folders that the Report Builder application should not display for the Role's targeted Entity, when the particular Role is used to reach the Entity. For example, the *AddressType* Attribute should be hidden when Address is displayed by using the *HomeAddress* Role but should be visible when the Entity is reached using another Role. This Collection is important when an Entity can be reached by different Roles and should show a different behaviour dependant on which Role was used to get to this Entity.

4.5.9 ExpandInline

The property indicates that the Report Builder application should not show the Role to the information worker. Using this setting all the fields of the related Entity are displayed instead as if they were part of the parent´s Entity. The default value of the property is false.

This behavior allows yet another approach for the de-normalization of data. The usage of this feature is recommended when you are confronted with the scenario, that in the source system the information for one Entity is split into two Tables (like Contact and AdressInfo) for storage or data-modeling purpose. The second Table does not represent an own Entity, it contains just Attributes for the other Entity.

By using expand inline and hiding the source Entity of the Attributes the developer can merge these two distributed structures into one Entity in the Report Model.

Role expansion is favoured over the lookup behaviour of an Entity when both are specified on the same object.

4.5.10 PromoteLookup

The property defines that the Report Builder client application, when the containing Entity is displayed as a lookup, also displays the target Entity as a lookup. This value is allowed only if the Role's containing Entity and target Entity are both lookup entities. Lookup Roles on the related Entity of a lookup Role are promoted if the value of PromoteLookup is true and the promoted Role's related Entity is not the Entity to which the Role is being promoted or one of its direct ancestors or descendents. The default value is defined as false.

4.5.11 Preferred

The property defines that Paths containing this Role should be preferred over Paths that do not contain preferred Roles. This optional Boolean property, that defaults to false indicates which path should be used in a preferred manner to reach another Entity when there is more than one possible path of roles that connect two Entities from which to choose.

4.5.12 Recursion

The property defines whether the relationship the Role relies on should be traversed recursively by default. Recursion is allowed only if the containing Entity is the same as the target Entity. Roles are recursively expanded, but the recursion stops when an attempt is made to expand items from Entity A into the context of A, or one of its direct ancestors or descendents.

4.5.13 Binding

The property describes the database object that represents this Role. Note that the specified end of the relation must bind to Columns in the Table to which the Entity containing the RelatedRole element is bound, or equal to the Column to which that Entity is bound. The other end of the relation must be in the Table to which this Role's containing Entity is bound, or equal to the Column to which this Entity is bound. Binding is required unless this Role's Entity is bound to a Table that contains the Column to which the RelatedRole's Entity is bound (or vice versa). In this case, the containment relationship between the Column and the Table is implied by their names, and the binding is not specified.

- CubeDimensionBinding
- DbDimensionBinding
- RoleOrigin

4.5.14 Hidden

This optional property defines weather the Information worker can see this Role in Report Builder client or not. The property is optional; if it is not set it defaults to false.

4.6 Filters

Any Attribute, no matter if it is an Expression or natively based on a database-field that is of Boolean DataType can have its IsFilter property set to true. If this is done it can be used as named Filter in any filter collection in Model Designer as well as on report Builder Client. To get an impression how this function works go to chapter 6.7

4.7 Expressions

Expressions stand for a set of Formulas in a Report Model that are used to define a new object or Attribute of an object.

In Report Models, the behavior of Expressions can be anchored or non-anchored. An anchored expression is only meaningful within a specific Entity context. For example, suppose you have an Entity called Customer and you have fields for Age and Salary and you create a new field called *SalaryAgeRatio* for each customer. Your expression might look like this: SalaryAgeRatio = Salary/Age. This expression is anchored within the context of the Customer Entity and is only useful in this context.

A non-anchored expression is an expression that can be meaningful within more than one Entity context. For example, suppose you have two entities called Customer and Orders. For every customer, there are multiple sales amounts. If you create a new field that displays the Total Sales for each customer, the expression for your field might look similar to this: [Customer] = Sum([Customer to Order]Amount).

Using Attributes and Entities in an expression earns an anchored one, whereas Literals, Nulls, AggregateAttributes, and ParameterRefs lead to a non-anchored expression. Functions are anchored if any argument within the expression is anchored.

4.7.1 Expression Builder GUI

The definition of an Expression is supported by an own GUI in Model Designer which looks like the following screenshot:

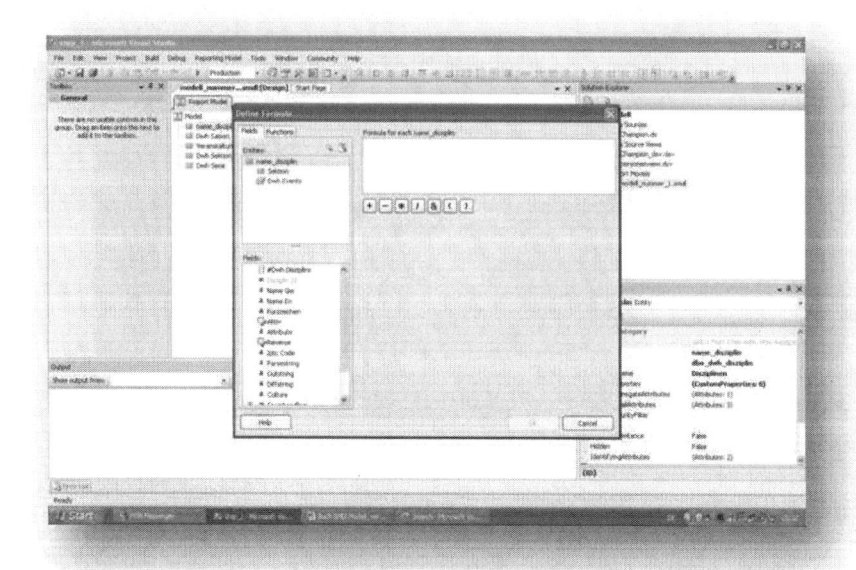

Image 10: Expression Builder GUI

In the left handed pane the developer can choose if he or she desires to access Entities and Attributes using the Entities-Navigation (the Navigation – Paradigm that Microsoft chosed is described in chapter 6.3). The developer can take one of the Entities or Attributes and transfer them into the Formula – textbox using drag & drop or by double clicking on the Object. Depending on the advanced/not advanced setting you can see just Roles with cardinality One or all Roles of an Entity If your Report Model is big and you are not sure in which Entity which Attribute is located Model Designer helps you with a Search-Window that opens on a click on the magnifier. This Window allows you to search for an Attribute by name und retrieves not just the found Attributes but also the information in which Entity it is contained.

When switching to the Functions Tab, the developer is presented with all the available functions (that are described on the following pages) in a grouped Tree-Structure. You cannot drag one of these functions into the formula window. The only way to accomplish this task is to double-click on it – then the function with hints appears in the formula - textbox.

In the right upper part is the formula textbox. It supports using the functions and objects of the left hand pane by using the moue as well as direct text editing.

One nice gimmick appears if you double - click on an Attribute in the formula textbox. In this case an expanded Formula for the Attribute is displayed. In this place the developer can accomplish these two tasks:

- **Aggregate to here:** If you double-click a field name displayed in the Formula box, the relationship between the primary entity and the field's entity are displayed. Click to apply an aggregate to the expression anywhere along the model path.
- **Apply a Filter:** out of the box there is no Filter defined. If you click on this link you can define a new filter that is applied on the Attribute used in the particular Expression. How to define a filter is described in chapter 4.6.

Below this textbox are buttons for the logical functions bound to buttons that work on button-click.

Besides the usage in a Report Model it is also possible to use Expressions directly in Report Builder client. This feature is not yet documented and the GUI of Report Builder client does not provide the Information worker with an editor like Model Designer, but if the value of a textbox (not a column in a table or cell in a matrix layout !) begins with = it is treated as an Expression that is evaluated at the runtime of the Report. For example, you can display the execution - time of the Report using the following Expression: =Globals.ExecutionTime.ToString("f"). But be aware that the possibilities are not that high, for example if you plan to use it to display Page-Numbers – that won´t be possible as the Report Header and Report Footer Section are not accessible in Report Builder.

4.7.2 Report Functions

Expressions, Formulas and Filters can be written in a VB Script like syntax. In the following pages I will describe the functions from an informational and usability standpoint; for detailed descriptions about the syntax and usage parameters please refer to the Books Online.

4.7.2.1 Aggregate Functions

Aggregate functions are used to perform calculations on a single value or a set of values to return a single (aggregated) value. The aggregate functions can use the following data types as input: DateTime, Integer, Decimal, Float, EntityKey, String, or Numeric.

- **AVG:** Calculates the arithmetic mean of all values in the provided set. NULL values are ignored in the calculation.
- **COUNT:** This function returns the absolute number of items in the set as an integer value. Be aware that NULL values are ignored by this function.
- **COUNTDISTINCT:** This function returns only the number of distinct items in a set as an integer. Also in this function NULL values are ignored.
- **MAX:** Delivers the maximum value in a set. This function ignores NULL values and is also capable of handling strings (they are ordered according to the defined collation-setting of the source database) by a string-ordering.
- **MIN:** Delivers the minimum value in a set. This function ignores NULL values and is also capable of handling strings (they are ordered according to the defined collation-setting of the source database) by a string-ordering.
- **STDDEV:** This function returns the standard-deviation (disparage of data)

assuming the input – set represents a sample of the whole population. NULL values are not considered in this calculation. Strings and Boolean values cannot be used as input for this function as they cannot be transferred into statistical meaningful numbers.
- **STDDEVP:** This function is the counterpart to the previous one, it works in exactly the same way, with the exception that it assumes the input – set is the whole population.
- **SUM:** returns the arithmetic sum of the provided set, so it is obvious it can't be used on String data. NULL values are ignored respective count as zero.
- **VAR:** This function returns the variance assuming the input – set represents a sample of the whole population. NULL values are not considered in this calculation. Strings and Boolean values cannot be used as input for this function as they cannot be transferred into statistical meaningful numbers.
- **VARP:** This function is the counterpart to the previous one, it works in exactly the same way, with the exception that it assumes the input – set is the whole population.

4.7.2.2 Conditional Functions

Those functions are used to determine if there are some specific criteria met and to react on them. These are the typical if-then functions you may know from other programming languages and can be used on Boolean, DateTime, Integer, Decimal, Float, EntityKey and String data.
- **IF**: This function evaluates a given Condition that has to result in Boolean output and returns a value for both possible results (true-part and false-part).
- **IN**: This function evaluates if one item is contained in a set to test against. The

functionality is exactly the same as you get in T-SQL. But keep in mind that all members of the set you are testing against have to be literals (so you probably have to do some conversions before) and the set may not be empty. Boolean values and Entity Keys are not permitted in the set.

- **SWITCH:** the SWITCH – function acts as enhancement to the previous IF – function. In the IF – function you could just evaluate a true/false check. In the SWITCH function you can test your value against a large number of conditions where the output of the first one that evaluates true is returned.

4.7.2.3 Conversion Functions

This set of functions provides you with the means to convert one DataType into another. These functions work for numeric and text DataTypes only.

- **INT** converts a given (numeric) value into an Integer.
- **DECIMAL** converts a given (numeric) value into a decimal DataType with a given precision.
- **FLOAT** converts a given (numeric) value into a decimal DataType with a given precision
- **TEXT** converts a numeric value into a String (acting like the ToString() function in .NET), for example to concatenate it with another String for display purposes.

4.7.2.4 Date and Time Functions

These functions give a broad range of calculations, extractions and splits that can be done on dates and times. Date and Time functions can use the following data types: String, Integer, and DateTime.

Their default format and specific behaviour is determined by the computer locale settings.

- **DATE:** this function acts more like a conversion – function. For a given day, month and year it returns a DateTime DataType with the time-portion set to 12:00 AM.
- **DATEADD:** returns the Date when, for a given start date a number of a given interval is added. The interval – identifier is not case sensitive and must be surrounded by quotation marks. Valid Intervals that can be added are year, quarter, month, week, day, hour, minute, second.
- **DATEDIFF:** returns the difference between two DateTime values in a given interval. For valid intervals refer to DATEADD.
- **DATETIME**: This function is an enhancement of the DATE function, as it does exactly the same job but enhances the previous function by accepting also hour, minute and second as parameters.
- **DATEONLY** is a stripping function as it only returns the Date – part from a given DateTime and sets the Time – part to 12:00 AM. This function is very useful if you have time – specific data and you only want to compare it by its date – part.
- **DAY** extracts the day of a given DateTime as an Integer
- **DAYOFWEEK** returns the encoded day of week (1=Monday) for the day of a given DateTime.
- **DAYOFYEAR** returns the number of a day in a year (January 1 = 1) of a given DateTime as an Integer.
- **HOUR** extracts the hour of a given DateTime as Integer.
- **MINUTE** extracts the minute of a given DateTime as Integer.

- **MONTH** extracts the month of a given DateTime as Integer.
- **NOW:** This parameter less function returns the actual DateTime.
- **QUARTER** returns the quarter for a given DateTime as Integer.
- **SECOND** returns the second for a given DateTime as Integer.
- **TODAY:** This parameter less function returns the actual date with the time portion set to midnight (12:00 AM). So if you want to get an equivalent for the T-SQL getdate() function you will have to combine the TODAY and NOW function.
- **WEEK** returns the week for a given DateTime as Integer. The first week is determined by the culture of the Report Model the function is used on. Depending on the culture it may be the first full week, the first week with at least 3 days or the week that carries January 1st. To be sure which algorithm is used please refer to the culture and calendar documentation in the MSDN-Library.
- **YEAR** returns the year for a given DateTime as Integer

4.7.2.5 Information Functions

These functions return information about the user who is actually using or consuming the ad hoc Report. So this is a very interesting output for the definition of user-dependent report behaviour like filters or user-specific expressions.

- **GETUSERCULTURE:** This parameter-less function returns the language/locale of the user who is consuming the Report (for the available enumerations refer to 4.1.4)
- **GETUSERID**: This parameter-less function returns the name of the user who is consuming the report in the format domain/account.

Unfortunately it is not possible to get the Active Directory Groups the person is in (Member OF) in this Version of the product but with some tweaking and administrative permissions on the source database there is a way I describe in chapter 9.1.5.

4.7.2.6 Logical Functions

These functions are the glue between simple conditions and bring them together into a logical connection to decide how to handle cases and do a branching. Logical functions can only be performed on Boolean parameters or (Boolean) conditions returned by other functions.

- **AND** returns true if both logical parameters result in a true.
- **NOT** returns true if one of the contained Boolean parameters returns false. Instead of NOT it is also possible to use <> in a formula.
- **OR** returns true if one of the logical parameters result in true and only returns false if all parameters earn a false.

4.7.2.7 Math Functions

This set of functions delivers some very basic and reduced mathematic formulas that are commonly needed. These functions can be performed on float, decimal and integer values.

- **MOD:** returns the remainder after a number is divided by a numeric divisor. The sign of the remainder is always the same as the divisor.
- **ROUND:** Rounds a number to a specified number of digits from the decimal point. If the number of digits is greater than zero, the number is rounded to the specified number of decimal places. If the number of digits is 0, then the number is rounded to the nearest integer. If the number is less than 0, then the number is rounded to the left of the decimal

point. If the number to the right is between 0 and 4 Reporting Services rounds down, and if the number is between 5 and 9 it rounds up.
- **TRUNC:** Truncates a number to the number of digits specified. If the number is positive, the number is truncated to the right of the decimal. If the number is negative, the number is truncated to the left of the decimal.

4.7.2.8 Operator Functions

The Operator functions are used to calculate basic mathematical values. Besides their textual representation they can be used by common symbols. A number of them are exposed as a button in the Expression – management page in Model Designer.

In addition to the following functions there is not to be forgotten that you can use parenthesis in every place to encapsulate pieces of logic that have to be executed in a smaller context.

Operator functions can use all of the numeric DataTypes and in some special cases string and DateTime values

- **ADD (+)** is used to add two or more numeric values together and returns a numeric value.
- **DIVIDE (/)** is used to divide two numeric values and returns a numeric value. It is not allowed to divide by zero as this will raise an error.
- **EQUAL TO (=)** checks if two numeric, string or DateTime values equate and returns a Boolean value, marking equality or not.
- **EXPONENTATION (^)** is used to raise a given numeric value by a power and returns a numeric value.
- **GREATER THEN (>)** is used to check if one numeric value is greater than another. The return type is a Boolean value.

- **GREATER THEN OR EQUAL TO (>=)** is used to check if one numeric value is greater or equal to another and returns a Boolean value.
- **LESS THEN (<)** is used to check if one numeric value is less then another. The return type is a Boolean value.
- **LESS THEN OR EQUAL TO (<=)** is used to check if one numeric value is less or equal then another and returns a Boolean value.
- **MULTIPLY (*)** is used to multiply numeric values and also returns a numeric value.
- **NEGATE** is used to negate the sign of the value and returns a numeric value.
- **NOT EQUAL TO (<>)** checks if two values are not equal and returns a Boolean value indicating whether this condition is true or false.
- **SUBTRACT (-)** is used to subtract one or more numeric values from a start-value and returns a numeric value.

4.7.2.9 Text / String Functions

This set of functions is used to provide some means to manipulate string-values. These functions can, as the name implies, only be used on strings and will fail on all other Datatypes.

- **CONCAT (&)** appends one or more strings together and returns a string. This function can be used to concatenate values as well as literals (enclosed in quotation marks).
- **FIND** returns the first occurrence of a given string value in another term as an integer. If the string-value is not found this function returns 0. Be aware that this function returns a 1-based value (so the first possible occurrence is 1 and

not 0 like in other programming languages).
- **LEFT** returns the left portion of a value with a given length (integer) as a string.
- **LENGTH** returns the number of characters of a string as an integer value.
- **LOWER** converts the upper case characters in a string value to lower case.
- **LTRIM** erases any number of blanks in a string on the left side and returns the resulting string.
- **REPLACE** looks for a given string in a value and replaces it by another given string. The return-value s a string.
- **RIGHT** returns the right portion of a value with a given length (integer) as a string.
- **RTRIM** erases any number of blanks in a string on the right side and returns the resulting string. Strings in this manner have their source quite often in databases with fixed-length text Columns, where the remaining positions are filled with blanks.
- **SUBSTRING** returns a piece of a string-value given a start-position (remember it is 1-based !) and a length as a string.
- **UPPER** converts the lower case characters in a string value to upper case.

4.8 Evolving your Report Model over time

As the source systems of the generated Report Models change over time (schema changes, addition of fields, and deprecation of fields) and also the demand articulated against the already built Report Models grows sooner or later, you as a developer will have to enhance your Report Model to adapt to these new circumstances.

Keep in Mind that not every change in the underlying systems or the DataSource View might break existing Reports, but if the purpose of underlying objects is changed you might end up with working but incorrect Reports[8]. Assuming you are working on a Report Model project in Model Designer, one way to retrieve Changes in the underlying structure is to click the Refresh Data Source Button in the upper left pane of the DataSource View Designer. This will present you with a small report about structural changes (added and removed fields, changed constraints etc) in the source system.

But this feature cannot give information about changes in the usage of fields – but that is a problem that is shared with all other Reporting Solutions and can't be solved using a technical approach. For this problem an organisational/structural solution like the implementation of change management processes or metadata repositories is recommended (see footnote).

If your Report Model is built on a UDM you don't even have the chance to detect structural changes (there is no tool for it) so in that case you even more have to rely on correct change management processes and metadata repositories.

If there are already Reports out that are based on the Report Model you want to modify there are some properties you are absolutely not allowed to change. Violating that rule will likely break the existing Reports. Knowing this in a Report Model based on relational data you may change every property except the following list:

- **Entity:** ID
- **Entity:** Inheritance definition

- **Attribute:** ID
- **Attribute:** DataType

---

[8] If you want to retrieve the data-lineage of a specific field in a report Model trough all the possible steps Microsoft provides a metadata – intelligence tool that creates a kind of warehouse to give you the information which fields end in which objects.

- **Attribute:** IsAggregate property
- **Attribute:** membership in an Entity

- **Role:** ID
- **Role:** Cardinality
- **Role:** Definition of the related Role
- **Role:** membership in an Entity

If a field (and the Attribute based on it) or a whole Table (and the Entity based on it) is to be deprecated in the source database and may not be used any more you can change the hidden property. If it is set to true the existing Reports using the Attribute or Entity will still work, but the object won't be available when creating a new Report or modifying an existing one.

Using this approach just makes sure that these fields are not used any more. But it gives you no information which Reports are deployed that are using this field already. In this case a Report Model based on the Reporting Services Database as I point out in 9.3.1 may be an interesting Management Tool to implement.

4.9 Publishing a Report Model

4.9.1 Build a Report Model Project

The Build command in Model Designer does a validation of the existing smdl – files in the opened project to make sure they accord to all internal rules before publishing them.

4.9.2 Deploy a Report Model

A Report Model can be deployed manually using some tools as well as programmatically accessing Report Builders Webservice.

- **Report Manager:** Uploading a .smdl file is equivalent to publishing a Report Model, which is possible if information about the DataSource is already available on the Report Server. This is the case with Analysis Services Models and Report Models that already have been published (based on a shared DataSource) using another tool. In Report Manager select the Upload File

button from the toolbar, select the Model File and click OK.
- **SQL Server Management Studio:** This tool provides the same possibilities and limitations for a Report Model upload as the Report Manager.
- **Business Intelligence Studio or Visual Studio:** For Report Models, which are built on a relational database model, the Model Designer is not just the tool to define and edit the Report Model, but also the tool to publish the output to a Reporting Server. In the Project-properties of the Report Model project the developer can define the TargetDataSouce Folder, the TargetModel Folder and TargeServer URL to deploy to. Once you click on deploy as a first step the DSV – Information is merged into the connected smdl file and afterwards uploaded to the Reporting Server.
- **Using the Report Server Webservice directly:** To upload a Report Model (remember it is only possible for a Report Model that applies to the Rules of a Report Manager Upload) using the Webservice use the following code:

```
Dim rs as new ReportingService2005
rs.URL = <enter URL of Report Server>
rs.Credentials = System.Net.CredentialCache.DefaultCredentials

dim fs as FileStream
fs = File.OpenRead(<enter path to SMDL file>)
dim modelDefinition as Byte() = new [Byte](fs.Length) { }
fs.Read(modelDefinition, 0, CInt(fs.Length))
fs.Close()

Try
    Rs.CreateModel(<enter ModelName>, "/", modelDefinition, nothing)
Catch e as SoapException
    <handle the exception>
End try
```

4.9.3 Associate a Report Model with a DataSource

After a Report Model has been successfully deployed to a Report Server the Report Model has to be associated with a DataSource that is to be used to access the source data. This can be done using Report Manager or Management Studio using the DataSource Property of the published Report Model. Keep in mind that only shared Data sources on the Report Server can be used for this purpose.

It is also possible to accomplish this task by code. The following sample code (added to the previous one) describes how to define a DataSource on an Analysis Server and associate it with the previous published report Model.

```
Dim dsDefinition as new DataSourceDefinition
dsDefinition.Extension = "OLEDB-MD"
dsDefinition.CredentialRetrival = CredentialRetrivalEnum.Integrated
dsDefinition.Connectionstring = <enter Connection String>
dsDefinition.ImpersonationUserSpecified = True
dsDefinition.Enabled = True
dsDefinition.EnableSpecified = True
Try
    rs.CreateDataSource (<enter DS name>, "/", False, dsDefinition, noting)
Catch e as SoapException
    <handle the exception>
End try
```

```
Dim ds() as DataSource
ds = rs.GetItemDataSources(<enter Model name>)
dim dsref as new DataSourceReference
dsref.Reference = <enter DS name>
ds(0).Item = dsref
Try
    rs.SetItemDataSources("<enter Model name>, ds)
Catch e as SoapException
    <handle the exception>
End try
```

5 Generating your first ad hoc Report in 5 Minutes

Report Builder client is the tool Microsoft provides in this release of SQL Server to give a group of users, referred to as Information Workers, the possibility to create and edit ad hoc Reports with.

As this tool is targeted towards business users it uses an abstraction layer, called Report Model to present the information structure in a business-related way to the user, hiding the technical terms from him or her. The internals, structure, creation and management of a Report Model were covered in Chapter 4 already.

If you are now eager to start Report Builder client you will not locate it in your Start-Menu at a first glance, even if you installed all the available components of SQL Server 2005. The reason of this behavior is that this application is provided as a so called Click-once application (more on this topic in chapter 6). You have to start Internet Explorer on the client you want to run Report Builder client on and navigate to the Report Manager Website (usually http://yourserver/reports) of a Report Server in your Enterprise that has Report Builder access enabled. To make this first introduction easy I advise you to start Report Builder client off the same Server the Report Model you intend to use resides on.

If your login has sufficient permissions (see Chapter 7 for more information on this topic) you will find a Button to launch Report Builder in the upper right area of the Website.

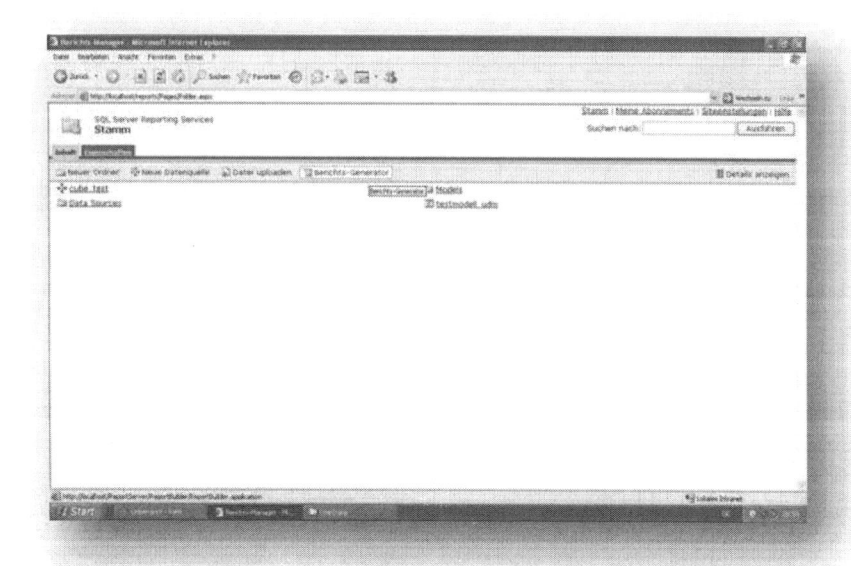

Image 11: Start button for Report Builder client (localised in German: Berichts-Generator)

After the Report Builder application is downloaded to your client (the first download may take some time), installed and started you are presented with a *first steps* window that requires you to select a Report Model[9] (if you worked your way through the book there should be some published Report Models already) and a template of the structure of your planned Report you are about to build. In this release of the product there are only three templates (Table, Matrix and Chart) contained in Report Builder client. I do recommend you have a clear picture in this stage about the type of Report you want to create as it is not possible le to change the type of the Report later on.

After you selected the Report Model and one of the three available templates (I would refer you to choose the Table as easiest to start with) you can see a navigation area containing the Report Model's items at the left and a Report-Design area on the right side.

In this design area which takes most of the space on the screen the blueprint of a Table (if you chosed this template) is visible and ready

---

[9] A Report Builder Report can only be based on one Report Model.

for you to work with. To give the Report you are editing a title as the first action to take click into the title bar above the Table blueprint and type in a name. After that task is finished you can start designing the data – content of the Report by dragging whole Entities or Attributes (of Entities) from the left-handed navigation area on to the design surface. After you dropped the first item on the design surface the contents of the left handed navigation pane changes. From now on Report Builder only displays the objects that have a logical connection (a Role defined in the Report Model) to the already used object and only gives you the option to navigate the paths that are defined in the Report Model.

On the design surface there is no real preview – data shown and the cells are only filled with placeholders and not live-data as in this stage the underlying database is not accessed. Only if you click on the Preview button the generated Report is rendered using real data.

Report Builder supports common features like filtering, sorting and grouping which will be described later on in Chapter 6.

Finally you can choose to save the Report (using the save-command in the Menu-bar) to the file system if you plan to work on the Report later without publishing it yet, or save it to a Report Server. If you save to a Report Server the Report is published and can be accessed by people who are granted view – permissions on the particular folder on the Report server where the Report is located. To render the Report these users do not need Report Builder on their client as the Report Builder Reports are displayed in Report Manager Website or a .NET Report Control just like the standard Reports you are used to from Reporting Services.

6 The Report Builder Client

6.1 Starting the Application

The Report Builder Application is a ClickOnce Application. That means it is not directly installed on a local Client, but it is downloaded from an URL and launched from the local Application Cache (C:\Documents and Settings\username\Local Settings\Apps\2.0\obfuscated directory). To run Report Builder client you need to have and use Internet Explorer (to navigate to the URL) and .NET Framework 2.0 or higher on the Client. Trying to open Report Builder with another Browser (for example Firefox) makes the Browser (locally) save the application and trying to open it afterwards. As the location where Firefox temporary saves this application is not the path mentioned above you will get an error message of missing support files when trying to start Report Builder, so yes Internet Explorer is absolutely needed in this case unless you remember the path where to save the application correctly. The deployment system checks if the .NET Framework (Version 2.0 or higher) is installed already, and if it is not the User is redirected to a download Site to install it first.

To launch Report Builder client, there are two URLs available:

- http://servername/reportserver/reportbuilder/reportbuilder.application: this URL opens Report Builder in Full Trust mode.
- http://servername/reportserver/reportbuilder/reportbuilderlocalintranet.application: this URL opens with Local Intranet permissions only

Report Builder client can be launched with a number of parameters that pre-define the behaviour slightly. Up to SP2 these parameters are documented and used by the tool. There might be more parameters (especially with upcoming Service packs) but they are not documented anywhere:

- **Report (ReportItem):** If you append the path to an already existing report (.application?/folder/reportname) to the calling URL

the specified Report will be loaded and opened for editing once Report Builder client is opened.
- **Model:** Append the name of the Report Model to the query string model calling URL (.application?model=/folder/modelname). This setting automatically opens the Report Builder client with a blank Report using the pre-selected Report Model and the Design - style for a tabular Report. It is not possible (at least with the documentation and settings I found) to define another Report template in the parameter.
- **Perspective:** If you append the Identifier (of the perspective to the above used Model path (.application?model=/folder/modelname &perspective=perspectiveID) Report Builder client is directed to one Perspective of a Report Model. Keep in mind that in this case you have to supply the ID (the GUID) of the Perspective and not the name of it. If the Perspective does not exist you will get an error-message.
- **Savelocation:** This parameter is new introduced with SP2 (Sharepoint Integration) and is fired if you open Report Builder client out of the Sharepoint Reporting Portal. The parameter ((.application?savelocation=path) tells Report Builder client where in Sharepoint the generated Reports should be saved. This parameter is mutually exclusive with the Report or Model parameter and is ignored if those are supplied

As Report Builder is a ClickOnce Application, it is started under the account of the actually impersonated User activating the URL mentioned earlier. If, for some reasons you don't want to have the application running under the currently logged on user, I will present you some scenarios in chapter 9.2.1, that might solve your problem.

6.2 Where does Report Builder get its info from?

Right after the start of the application you are presented with a window that requires you to choose a Report Model to work with. Up to SP1, Report Models could only be chosen from the server you started Report Builder on. This Solution was not satisfying as it required multiple downloads and starts of the application if the Report Models resided on different Reporting Servers which is quite frequent in larger enterprises. With SP2 of Reporting Services 2005 the Information Worker now has the possibility to choose which Server he/she wants to access right in the opening-stage of Report Builder.

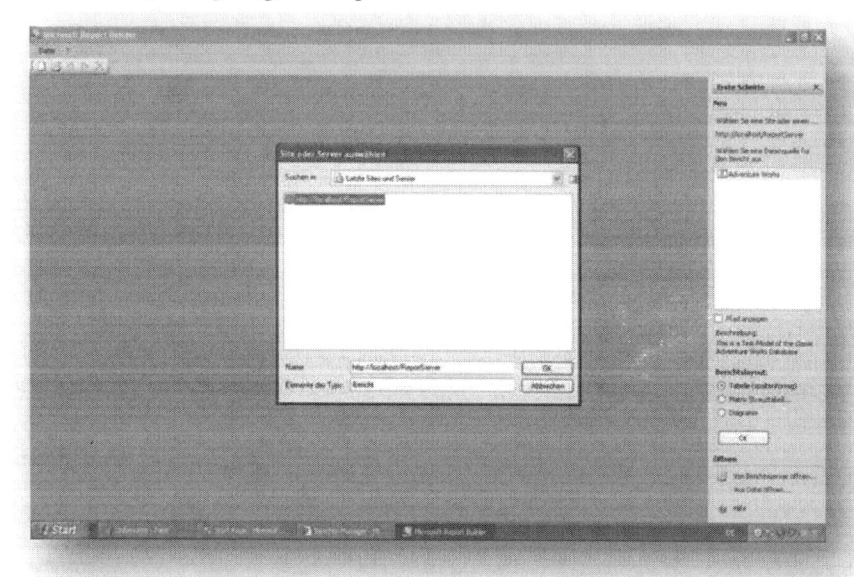

Image 12: selecting a Report Server in Report Builder client SP2

6.3 Data and Navigation in Report Builder

6.3.1 Report Builder Fields

Report Builder provides you with seven types of fields representing different types of data to fulfill your duty to create an ad hoc Report.

- **Text:** This type of field denotes textual data (strings) that carry literally no size limitation. Keep in mind that this data is rendered as pure text no matter what the content is. So URLs in this text will not be clickable and declarative information (like HTML - formatting) will be rendered as clear string.
- **Number:** This is the condensed type for numeric data, no matter if it carries a sign or if it is a float DataType or an integer. If the developer of the Report Model

enabled it you will find some sub-functions if you click on the + sign that is displayed to the left of the symbol representing the number. The numeric functions you possibly see are *Count* (represented by #), *Avg*, *Min* and *Max*.

- **Date & Time:** As the name suggests already this type carries Dates and/or Times. If the developer of the Report Model you are working on permitted it during Model generation you can access additional deferred subtypes clicking on the + sign left of the type. These subtypes may include *Day*, *Month*, *Year*, *Quarter*, *First* and *Last*.
- **Money:** stands for any numeric data with an assigned currency symbol.
- **Boolean:** stands for a Field that allows only two states (yes/no, true/false, 0/1).
- **Image:** This type represents binary data that Report Builder tries to render as a picture.
- **Aggregate:** This Field is not directly tied to a particular field in the underlying DataSource; it stands for a defined aggregation – formula (e.g. Sum, Avg). If you are using this field in a Report you will soon realize it is the only field which outcome is depending on other fields of the Report.

6.3.2 Report Builder Navigation

In the left/top part of Report Builder client is a navigation-area located that allows you to move through the contents of a Report Model. If you assume that this works like many other Navigation-tools you know already you will be surprised, as I lined out in Chapter 5 already. Microsoft chose a new paradigm to make Navigation for Information Workers easier and more convenient. The solution chosen may look confusing in the first point but really is a nice enhancement on the long term.

Immediately after the Report Model is loaded this Navigation-structure acts just like any classical flat list that displays the available Entities of the Report Model.

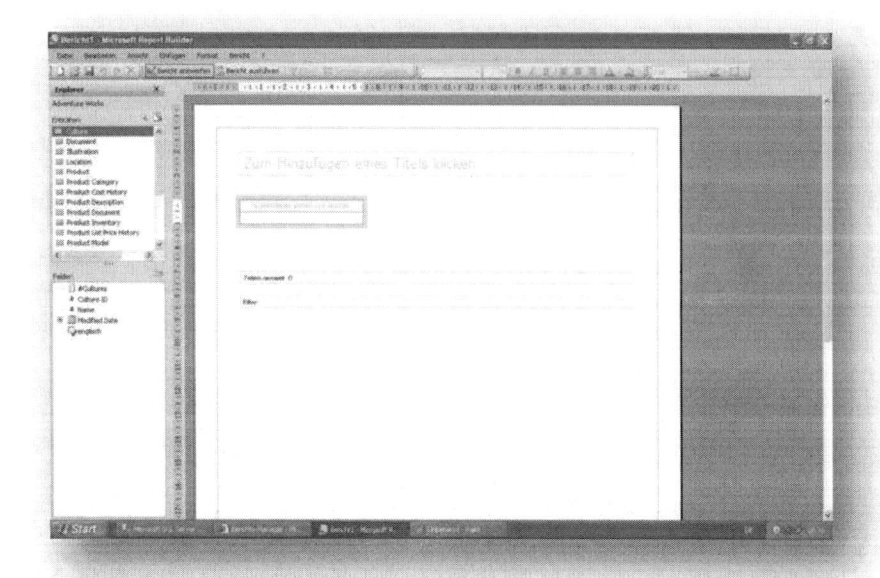

Image 13: Data Navigation in its initial state

Just after you drag the first field on the Design-surface of Report Builder client to start designing your Report, the list will change its layout and behavior. From that point on the Navigation displays itself as an auto-collapsing tree with recursive elements to navigate on. These elements are only visible if you switch to the extended navigation using the Menu View/extended Explorer or by toggling the Icon right to the search icon. This structure gives you the opportunity to navigate up and down in the presented structure in using the logical references that are persisted in the Report Model.

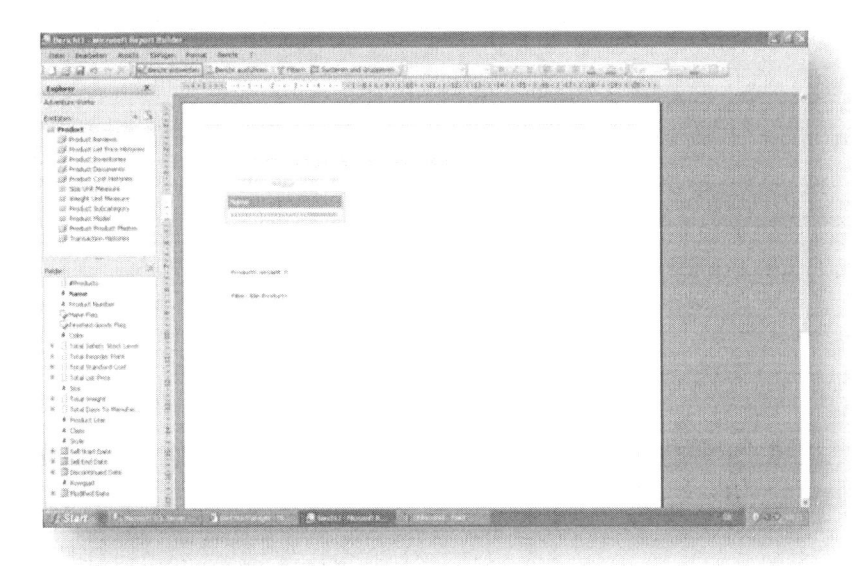

Image 14: Data Navigation in its tree – state

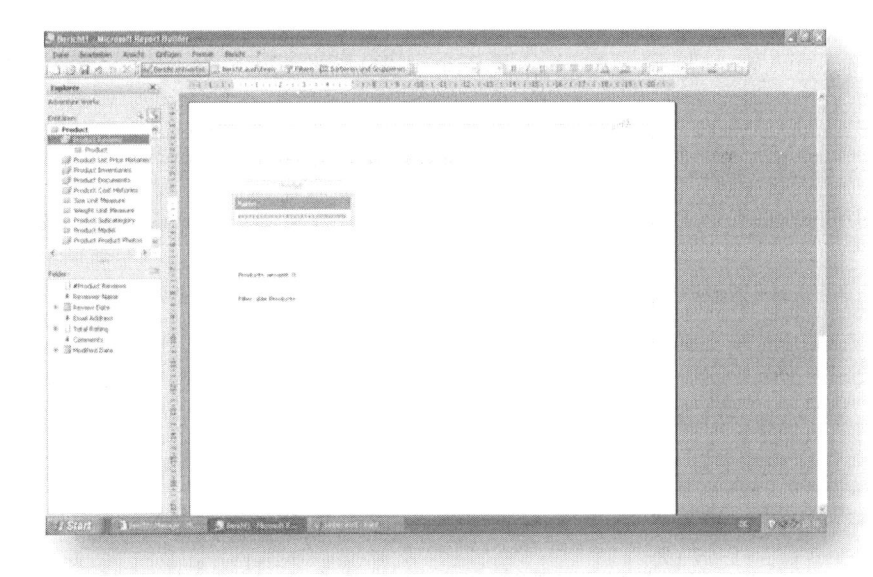

Image 15: Data Navigation in its tree – state showing the extended Explorer

In this mode the Navigation displays the Entities that can be reached from the particular Entity you just dragged onto the Design surface using the Roles that are defined in the Report Model. The key concept in this place is the relationship that builds up between these two Entities, as the second Entity is depended on the first one. For example in the image above the first Entity used is Products (I dragged the Product name on the Surface). The Navigation Explorer now only provides me with all the Entities that have a Role connecting with Products.

Given this approach there are two traps an Information Worker might fall into, especially if he or she has worked with other tools already and is not fully aware of this paradigm to design a Report and use the Navigation:
- Importance of the **first used Entity**: The first Entity you drag onto the Design surface in a new Report ends up as the primary Entity of the Report. In short word this means that Report Builder assumes your Report is fundamentally about this particular Entity. Thus using this Entity the navigation switches to just display the Entities that are connected with the primary Entity. But as a reminder for database – experts: this Navigation does not represent the relations of the underlying database, as you might realize in the following point the power of Report Builder reaches further than that. Keep an eye on the Design Surface during your design work since the primary Entity might change as you drag other Entities on the surface, depending on the elements you pull in and the position you choose (more on this issues is described in the Grouping section later on in this chapter)
- Dependency on the **order the Entities are used**: It really gets interesting on the one hand and a bit confusing on the other hand once you realize that using this approach allows you to

go anywhere in the Report Model using this Navigator, even back to the Entity you started from. But you have to keep in mind that the path you use to navigate through the Report Model defines the structure of the Data you request. For example (thanks to Bob Meyers for the example), the path *Customer* → *Orders* → *Employee* → *Territory* → *Employees* → *Orders* → *OrderDetails* → *Products* represents the products from each order detail of each order taken by the employees in the same territory as the employees that took the orders of this customer. Seems a bit confusing at first, but once realized this navigation-paradigm bears a great potential.

One common observation I do want to share in this place. Sometimes a Report Model is enhanced by an additional Entity and the Information worker who uses it or wants to use it complains he or she does not see the recently added Entity in Report Builder client. In the most cases this trial (checking if the desired Entity is already available in the report Model) is done on an existing Report and the Information worker does not realize that the new Entity can only be found in the correct connection-path of the sources already used in the Report and is not visible by default. If you are testing the deployment of a new Entity I always recommend using a "fresh" Report to verify if the changed elements work as expected.

One feature to mention in this place is a search utility Microsoft provides if you are looking for a particular Object and the Report Model is too big to find it easily. In the Report Menu (or by clicking on according symbol in the Navigation window) the there is a Search-Window that allows you to enter the name or the part of a name of an object you are looking for. The results-table gives you all the hits, not just with the names of the Objects but also their containing Entity.

6.4 Creating and editing a Report

A Report Builder Report is a XML-Structure, defined in RDL (Report Definition Language) likewise the Reports that have been built in Report Designer. Although both RDL – Files are based on the same XML - Schema, Report Builder is only capable to use a subset of the elements Report Designers can dwell in.

As it will be viable in this chapter that the functionalities of a Report Builder Report differ somewhat from a Report Designer Report so on the one hand there are some limitations in the RDL and on the other hand there are some extensions that are not available in Report Designer (for example Click-Trough)

Report Builder is the client-side tool Microsoft provides out of the box for an Information Worker to build ad hoc Reports but it is not limited to this tool. As the generated Report is a XML-File the Report itself also can origin from different tools (3rd Party or self programmed).

- **Create a new report**: To create a new Report you either can use the wizard that initially pops up when you launch Report Builder client or you can click on *File/New* or the *New*-Symbol of the menu to open the according wizard. This wizard I described earlier already requires the Information Worker to choose a Report Model (or a Perspective of it) and a Report Template the report will be based on. These settings are absolutely exclusive and cannot be changed later on.

- **Open a report (from file)**: In Report Builder client previously generated Reports can be opened for editing from different sources. Usually (with an exception covered in Chapter 8.6). The Information Worker can only open RDL-files that were built according to the rules of Report Builder; otherwise Report Builder client will state an error. To open a Report click on *File/Open* in the Menu to load a Report from your local file system. By clicking on *File/Open* you get a familiar file-open dialog which gives you the choice to open a Report from a Report Server or, new with SP2, from a Sharepoint[10] 2007 server.

---

[10] To be able to access Reports saved in a SharePoint library the Report Server needs to be configured for SharePoint integrated Mode. How to accomplish

The only requisite to keep in mind is that the Report Model used to generate the Report needs to be available in the place it was located once the Report was created. So be aware that you cannot choose a different Report Server (without also moving the Report Model to this place) in this place as you already defined the targeted Server in the step before when you committed yourself to a Server already by choosing a Report Model.

- **Save a Report (to file):** You can save a Report to the same locations you could open one by using the according Options in the File Menu. The only limitation to keep in mind is that you need to have at least one Entity or Attribute contained in the Report, otherwise you can´t save it as it is not possible to save an empty report.

6.4.1 Report Templates

In Report Builder the Information worker initially has to choose one Report Template that defines the Style that is used to build an Ad - hoc Report. In the actual Version of Report Builder there are three Templates available that cannot be modified or otherwise be adapted, as the information is stored directly in the binaries of Report Builder:

- **List/Table Report:** generates a Report that contains one Table structure with the Columns defined out of the Attributes and each row representing one instance of an Entity.
- **Matrix:** creates a Report that contains a dynamic Table where both axes can be defined by using Attributes and the remaining value-are is populated by the instances of the retrieved Entities.
- **Chart:** creates a Report that displays as an Excel-like Chart – graphic.

In this version of Report Builder client there is no possibility to have a mixed Report, for example containing a Table and a Chart. It is also not possible (as lined out already) to modify

---

this task is described in http://msdn2.microsoft.com/en-us/library/bb283151.aspx

the Templates as they are directly encoded in Report Builders binaries or to use subreports. If you have, for example the demand to add a company-logo or a disclaimer to a published report you will have to modify it during the upload/storage on Report server. An overview on possible approaches how to do that will be presented in Chapter 9.2.2

6.4.2 General Report Properties

In the Report – properties window (click *Report* in the Menu and choose *Report Properties*) the Information worker can define some properties that specify how the end user is able to interact with the Report that is created once it is published:

- **User Sorting:** If this option is set (default), the end user is allowed to sort the retrieved data on his or her own by using the little up/down arrows that will be automatically generated in the HTML view when the Report is consumed in Report Manager or the Report Control. For more information on this feature refer to Chapter 6.9.
- **Drilltrough:** If this option is set (which is the default) to true the generated Report (if published) can act as a target to drilltrough from another Report. With selecting this option you enable the definition of the drilltrough context and drilltrough Source Query parameter that have to be defined by the administrator of the Report Server when configuring the drilltrough capabilities. To allow the drilling to this particular Report the administrator has to set the Entity the Report stands for in Management Studio (which only works after this option is set). Keep in mind that this parameter can only be set an a Server running the Enterprise Edition of SQL Server 2005, the other versions (which do not support drilltrough) do not give you the option to define this parameter correctly
- **Fixed headers:** This option, which is also enabled by default, fixes headers if the user has to scroll through a large Report so they are always visible on the screen in the HTML-View. This setting

affects headers of a Table as well as headers and row-descriptions of a Matrix.
- **Drilldown:** If this option is enabled, which is the default it is possible to show and hide subgroups in a Matrix – Report using the + and – sign. In Reports based on one of the other Templates this option is grayed out.
- **Server Totals:** If this option is checked the end user or Information worker gets access to calculated totals where he or she does not have access to the underlying fields. This option assures that by using this feature the totals the user is allowed to see are generated on the server, so no sensitive data the user may not access is transferred behind the scenes.

6.4.3 Page Properties (Page Layout)

If you open the Report properties window of Report Builder client using *File/Page properties* most of the options presented to you will look quite familiar to a Microsoft Office-user, so I will only supply a short summarization of these settings assuming you know how to use and define them.

- **Margins:** These settings give you the possibility to define the distance between the edges of the page (for printed Reports) to the usable drawing surface for each of the four sides.
- **Paper Size:** This selection gives you the option to either choose a known paper format (from a list) or to enter a custom format using Width and Height information to be that basis for layouting Reports for printout.
- **Page Orientation:** This setting defines weather the orientation of the Report the Information worker is creating is Portrait (the page is longer vertically) or Landscape (the page is longer horizontally).
- **Page units:** This is the place that defines weather the numeric information entered is handled as inches or centimeters. Report Builder client tries to guess the optimal setting by using the local culture

the client is running on, but you are free to change it to your needs in this place.

- **Grid:** The Information worker can define the Grid as a helper for layouting the Report by defining the grid spacing to his or her demand. If every object is to aligned to the Grid select the *Snap to grid* checkbox. As there is literally no possibility in Report Builder to position or size the report elements by numeric values the Grid remains as the only possibility to support layouting a Report.

6.5 Designing a report

This chapter covers some of the general design-elements and properties of a Report Builder Report that are not dependant on the type of data retrieved or the template chosen.

6.5.1 Titlebox, Filterbox and Row Count

When generating a new ad hoc Report in Report Builder client the application adds three special Textboxes to the Design surface per default. The **Titlebox**, which is initially formatted in Arial 18 pt, can be positioned on any position of the Report and can be edited in any way it is needed. One shortcoming to point out is that it is not possible to have a returning Titlebox for every page in the generated Report output; it only appears once on the spot you positioned it.

If you (accidently) deleted the Titlebox and need it later on it can be recreated by using the Mouse and right clicking on the Design surface, choosing *insert* and *Textbox* to add the Titlebox again.

The additional special Textboxes are a description of the **selected filters** on a Report (Filter description) and the **Number of returned rows** (Rowcount) which are displayed by default. It is not possible to manipulate the content of these Textboxes, but you are free to change the formatting to your needs as well as to delete this item. If you need to recreate them you can do it by using the same procedure as described for the Titlebox.

6.5.2 Report Background

The Design - options you have on the Background of a Report Builder Report are limited to exactly one option. You can choose a color for the background but also this option is limited in Report Builder as you only have a limited subset of 40 colors, predefined by Microsoft available. No patterns and no gradients, just plain colors are possible. To define a color right click on the background, select the *Format* - Menu and select *Fill*, choose your color and click OK.

6.5.3 Images

If you need to enhance the Report you are generating by a company or department logo or other graphical support, starting with Service Pack 1 there is a possibility to position (external) images on the Report. But do not mix up this functionality with the handling of images returned from the DataSource which will be covered later on.

Actually the following formats can be successfully added as a static image:

- **BMP:** Windows Bitmap
- **JPG:** Joint Photographic Experts Group
- **GIF:** Graphics Interchange Format
- **PNG:** Portable Network Graphics
- **JPE:** Java-Python Extension

To add an image click *Insert/Image* or use the context sensitive menu (right mouse button) in the design surface of Report Builder client to accomplish this task. Navigate to the source in the opening dialog window and choose the needed image. By default the image is positioned with its original size in the upper left corner of the Report. Be aware: if there is another element at this position already it is not moved to accommodate the Image, so you have to make sure yourself that the elements do not overlap. It is also not possible to have the Image overlapping with one of the Template objects (Table, Matrix, and Chart). Although it may look like it is working correctly in Report Builder client (even in the Report Preview) there will happen some ugly rearrangements when opening the Report in Report Manager, so make sure there are no overlapping static images in your Reports.

The image is saved in the Report definition as byte array and the Mime-type information about its format.
To edit the image use the Format options or right click the image and choose the appropriate tabs in the appearing menu. In the upcoming Menu you can edit three settings:

- **Size:** In the sizing dropdown-list (found in the alignment tab) you can choose the mode how to resize the image (AutoSize, Clip, Size to fit, and Fit Proportional) and click OK. In the Design-Area you can use the handles on every side to resize the image to your needs. If you need to do some greater shrinking of images I recommend using an external tool and import the image again as an image saved in the Report definition keeps its file size although it may be cropped down.
- **Padding:** To define the padding of the image you have to choose the alignment tab. Now you can enter the desired distance (padding) for each of the four sides of the image (by default the padding is 0 points) measured in points to other objects on the design surface.
- **Border:** After choosing the Border tab you can define a border for your Image using the Settings (Style, Width, Line Color) you are familiar with from Microsoft Office.

6.5.4 Textbox

A Textbox is a Report Item that contains some Text. In difference to a Standard Report it is not possible to populate the content of this element out of the data source (in our case the Report Model). In Report Builder the content of a Textbox needs to be typed in at design time. To add a Textbox choose *insert/Textbox*, use the context-sensitive menu in the design area or drag it from the left-handed menu on the design surface.

The Textbox can be positioned on any place you like, just use the drag-border to accomplish this task. The drag points can be used to define the size of the object.

The Text in a Textbox is automatically broken according to the width of the Textbox. You also have to make sure you supply sufficient height for the Text. Using the Preview option is a good way to check the Report to see if your text boxes look proper.

6.5.5 Executing, exporting and printing a Report

To work with a Report (and its data) you are building in Report Builder client you need to execute (or preview) this Report. With this command you switch the surface so the Tool accesses the underlying database (defined in the Report Model) for the first time and retrieves and displays the data.

The complete Report is rendered, which may or probably will result in a multipage Report, so in this mode you have the possibility to browse through the pages.

Only out of this mode in Report Builder it is possible to export the Report in a rendering format or print it out, as in the design – mode only the structure of the Report without any content is defined, using the menu on the right click of the Mouse. To save the executed Report in another rendering format select *Export/Save* and use one of the supported formats.

Printing out a Report out of Report Builder works like in any other Office Application with the exception that this command is also only available on the right mouse click. You can choose a printer, define Margins, paper options, copies, etc and do the printout.

6.5.6 Rendering considerations

Report Builder Reports can be rendered to all the formats Reporting Services is capable of, even custom rendering extensions if you happen to have one of these. This chapter will not describe all the specifics of the rendering engine; in that case please refer to Reporting Services Literature. But there are some considerations to keep in mind for the Person (usually the Information worker) that defines a Report. As this person might not be a developer who had contact with Reporting services already I will outline some notes and considerations for the available standard Rendering Formats:

- **Excel (Excel 2003):** When a Report Builder Report is exported to Microsoft Excel it will try to generate a Worksheet that looks pretty much the same as the Report itself. As the Number of Worksheets is limited an overflow during the export generates an Error. Also keep in mind that Excel supports a maximum of 65536 rows and 256 Columns. If the exported Report exceeds this numbers an Error will be displayed.

An interesting fact is also that the maximum width of an Excel Column is 255 characters or 1726 points. This number is not checked during the export process and may lead to unexpected results. Also an Excel-cell may only contain 32767 characters; this number is also not checked during export.

The expressions in the Report are only exported with their Result and are not converted into an Excel-formula.

Diagrams are not exported as Excel-Diagrams you can work with and are stored as image in the Excel sheet.

An export in the Excel 2007 file format is not supported yet.

- **Web-Archive:** This export can generate a Web-Archive of Type HTML 3.2, HTML 4.0 or MHTML. All versions are generated using the UTF-8 Coding. All positions of elements in the Report are converted into CSS-Positions, where differences below 0,2 mm are treated as 0. The generated HTML in this version does not allow overlapping Elements. If elements overlap these are repositioned and may destroy your layout.

  A Matrix will be rendered as a Table; Textboxes are rendered as DIV – elements. Images are embedded as IMG Tags.

  Depending on the chosen HTML Versions there are some quite big differences in styling of the output, for his Information refer the help file of Report Builder.

- **Adobe Acrobat (PDF):** The generated File is a PDF version 1.3 but it is recommended to have at least Adobe Acrobat 6 on your machine. Be aware that the font you use to format the Report is also needed on the Report Server to generate the PDF-File correctly. As The Rendering Engine does not embed Fonts into the generated PDF also on the viewing clients the used Font has to be installed to display the Report correctly, otherwise the missing Font will be replaced by one of the Standard fonts. In PDF some Metadata is written automatically. It is Title (the Name Attribute of the Report), Creator (the Name and version of Reporting Services), Producer (the Name and version of the Rendering Extension) and the CreationDate.

Images that have been saved as JPEG in Report Builder are also exported as JPEG; all other Images are converted to PNG.

- **TIFF-Graphic:** This option allows exporting Reports as Graphic. Using GDI+ you have (using renaming and typing in the desired format) the Option to save the report also as BMP, EMF, GIF, JPEG and PNG. Microsoft has put in some Logic to put as much data as possible on one page and not to shred that Tables or Matrix more than absolutely necessary.
- **XML-Data:** The generated XML File is made up of a strictly defined Schema. The Root-node of the XML is the Report with Diagram, Matrix and Chart as siblings. Be aware that Images are ignored in this export completely.
- **CSV Data:** The first row of the generated File contains the Header of all Columns, in the next rows there are the rows, separated by a comma. Each Line is ended by a Line-Break (CrLf). If the exported Data is a Table at the End there is an additional Column that contains the number of rows of this Table. Formatting, layout and other Fields than the Data itself are ignored.

6.5.7 Formatting basics for Textboxes, Rows, Columns and Cells

- **Background Color**: Colors can be applied the whole Report, Textboxes, Charts or Cells. To apply a Background Color choose the desired Item and use *Format/Fill* and define the color to use. In Report Builder you have only a limited subset of 40 colors, predefined by Microsoft available. One thing to keep in mind – there is no "No-color" or transparent color. If you want to remove a coloring you have to choose white as the color. Compared to the Microsoft Office Products Report Builder has some limitations in this place as you cannot use patterns, gradients or other graphical effects as a background.

- **Fonts**: The Font-format of a Report Item (Textbox, Cell, and Diagram) can be formatted using *Format/Font* or the appropriate Symbol. You can define the Font-type (Name or Family), Font- styles, Size, Font-Color and the Line spacing as well as Font-effects like underline and strikethrough as well as the color of the font. As these settings are very familiar to Microsoft Office this topic will need no further explanation. Usually the Standard-Font of the most Items is Tahoma, sized 8 points.

- **Formatting numeric Data:** To format numeric data (Microsoft includes Money and DateTime also in this type) use the Number – tab of the Format – Dialog box which is only available if you try to format a Field containing numeric data. In this place you can define the number of decimals used (default is 2), add a Thousand Separator (weather it is a . or a , depends on your local settings), define the Currency Symbol (in case of a Money – Attribute) and define how negative Numbers are displayed. All these settings should be quite familiar from Microsoft Excel so I will not go into deeper details in this place.

- **Borders and Gridlines:** To apply a Border to an element choose *Border* in the *Format-Menu* and define a Linetype (None to remove all Borders, Outline to display o Border around the selected Element or one of the four positions around the Element) ad set the line options like Style, Width and Color.

- **Aligning Report Items:** If you want to align Report Items to each other after you dragged them on the design surface the only option Microsoft provides is to use the Snap to Grid Option in the Page setup. Besides this aid it is up to you, the Information worker to assure the Items are well aligned together. Inside a cell the content can be aligned horizontally (left, right, middle) and vertically (top, middle, body) using the Format options of a cell. A cell also has a padding defined (standard 2 pts) that makes sure the content is not too close together. This padding can be tuned up to 10 pts.

I would like to mention a specific limitation in this place. If the content of an List- or Matrix Element is an HTML-Code or an URL Report Builder will neither be capable (at least in this version of the product) of displaying the HTML-formatting nor present you a clickable URL. In the case of the URL, and having an Enterprise Edition of SQL Server available you can overcome this limitation by using a specifically designed Drill trough Report (see 6.10.2).

6.5.8 Generating List and Matrix Reports

6.5.8.1 Using Images in a List or Matrix

Using images in a Report is straight forward in Report Builder client, you select the according field in the left pane and drag it on to the design surface/into the Table or matrix, and voila you are done.

This approach works nice and easy if you have the images stored inside the database as binary data type. But in a lot of cases inside the database only a reference path to the file system is stored and the application that uses the database has its own logic to retrieve the image. A possible solution for this scenario will be explained in chapter 9.2.3

6.5.8.2 Column width

The width of a column inside a List Report stays fixed and is not dynamically changed to accommodate the data retrieved while the Report is rendered. It is your responsibility as the Information worker to choose the size wisely in terms of usability and readability of the Report output.

The width can only be changed by using the Mouse, positioning it at the edge of a column and dragging the width as soon as the cursor changes to the symbol indicating the possibility to change the size. Unfortunately Microsoft does not provide you with a possibility to use numeric values in this release of report Builder.

6.5.8.3 Row height

The height of a Row is dynamically calculated during the rendering of a Report based on the content inside this Row. You can adjust the (minimum) size of the rows to accommodate the data contained in the report. The way to accomplish this task is exactly the same as with the column width.

6.5.8.4 Freezed columns

In larger Reports you or the end user might encounter the problem when scrolling from left to right that the first/last columns are not visible. You can enhance the usability of a report by freezing columns, so these columns stay in place even if you scroll through the Report in HTML-View.

It is possible to start freezing columns from both edges, but it is obviously not allowed to have all columns freezed.

You can control the setting which columns or column groups are frozen by using the column markers on the top of the list like you can see in the following image.

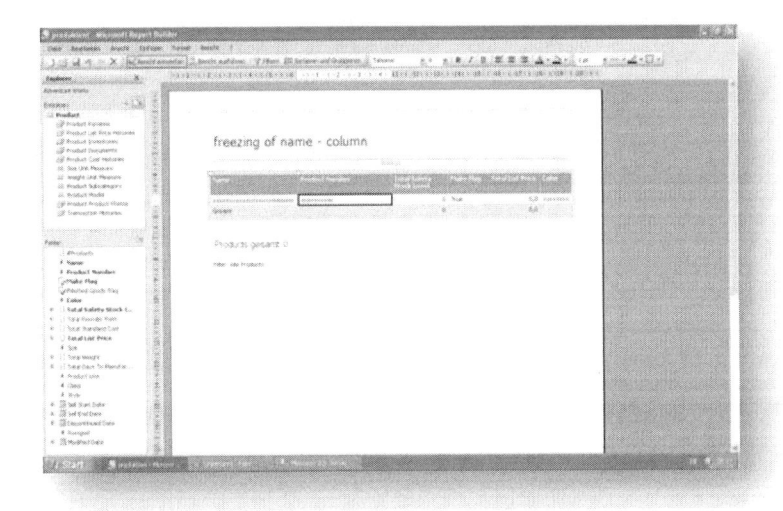

Image 16: frozen column in Report Builder client

6.5.9 Graphical Reports (Charts)

A Chart in Report Builder is rendered using the Dundas Charting Component in the background, so most of the features I will describe in this chapter will be familiar if you designed Diagrams in Microsoft Excel already, so I will keep the description as brief as possible to avoid repeating information.

You can drag the Fields into three different areas to define in which place of the Chart the information will show up:

- **Value group:** Defines the size of one Chart – element in a Category group. To get a Chart rendered, this group has to contain at least one Attribute, whereas dragging more than one Attribute to this area earns you one chart element per Attribute (or a combined element in case of stacked Chart types). Report Builder supports direct derived Fields as well as aggregate Fields in this area
- **Category group:** This group is used to define the individual groups of data and is usually represented by the X – Axis (for example in a Line-Chart or Box Chart). If you drag more than one Field into this area it

will result in a nested group. The value of the attributes contained in the category group will be displayed as the x-Axis measures. The nesting from general to specific corresponds with the direction up to down (right to left) in this group.
- **Series group:** This group defines the grouping of Data in a single point of a category and adds (if the Chart type supports it) the third dimension. The value of the fields contained in the series group will be represented in the Chart´s legend.

Concerning the sizing of Diagrams there are some differences. Whereas Report elements based on Lists or Matrixes adopt their size to the data returned, Diagrams do not act in that way, so it is your responsibility as an Information worker to size it correctly in Report Builder´s design mode.

6.5.9.1 Chart title

To add titles to a Chart or the used Axis right click the mouse on the Diagram – surface and edit the Titles as needed. One limitation dispositional of Report Builder is the fact that these Textboxes may not contain more than one line of text (no line breaks) and there is no way to rotate these Boxes. In the case of Axis titles it is just possible to align them with the Axis.

6.5.9.2 Data (Row) Marker

A Data Marker is an element of a chart that displays each data point the Chart is built of as a graphical element like a cross, circle or a bunch of other options. To add or remove a Data Row Marker right click with the Mouse on the DataRow you would like to edit, select *show Markers* and define which type of Marker to show as well as how to format it.

Additionally you can have a Label (called Data Point Label) on every one of these Marker points. To enable that right click on the DataRow once again and check the *Show point Labels* Checkbox.

6.5.9.3 Chart Legend

A Chart legend is a combined box that gives the end user of a Report the possibility to get a meaning of different series or value groups, depending on the chart style. A legend is shown by default every time you create a report based on the Chart – template, but you are free to move, delete and if needed recreate this element as needed.

To remove a legend right click on the chart, choose *Chart Options* from the menu, switch to the *Legend tab* and deselect the *Show legend* checkbox. To recreate select the Checkbox again.

The positioning of a legend is, compared to Excel, somewhat limited to a number of positions Microsoft allows. To do that right click on the chart, click on *Chart options* and on the *Legend Tab* select one of the possible positions provided in the dropdown list. If you dare to have the Legend being drawn inside the plot area select the according Checkbox in this place.

Finally to format the elements a Legend consists of right click on the chart once again, choose *Chart options* and switch to the *Legend tab*. Now you have the possibility to format the font, the borders and the background color of the Legend.

6.5.9.4 Chart Axes

A typically chart (I assume a bar chart for example) does have to Axes. On (the X-Axis) does carry the categories and is normally layouted horizontally, whereas the individual values are visible on the Y-Axis (often called value Axis). In a three dimensional Chart there is also a Z-Axis that is occupied by the Chart´s series.

You can format the Axis Labels in the same way you would expect it in Excel, but of course with some limitations in the Axis-Menu which will be described in the next paragraph.

By default the Axis of a Chart is displayed on the left side of the Chart. But if you want to have the position switched, there is a reversed Checkbox in the Axis Options (right click on the chart, choose Chart options and switch to the tab of the Axis to modify). Similar to this task you can also modify the point in which those two axis cross. By default it is the Minimum of both Axis, but in the Axis-menus you are free to enter the crossing – points for both axes. If you are using these two options together you should already get almost every scaling variety out of Report Builder you might need. Finally, when dealing with a big range of numbers it might be useful to switch an axis to a logarithmic scale. This task can be done by checking the according Checkbox in the Axis menu. Be advised in this place that there is no sign in the Chart that you are using a logarithmic scale, so it's your responsibility as an Information worker to make that clear to the end users if you use this option.

- **Gridlines** are horizontal or vertical lines, based on the Axis that enhances the readability of Charts in some cases. Like in Excel Microsoft provides Major and Minor gridlines. To enable or disable a Gridline right click on the chart, click *Chart Options* and on the *Tab of the axis* you want to enhance select or deselect the according checkboxes.
- **Tick marks** are the little markers that are shown for each interval you define on an Axis. To define the interval right click on the chart, click *Chart Options* and on the *Tab of the axis* you want to modify and enter a number into the interval input field.
- **Scale:** Defines the granularity of the Axis, like in Excel. Report Builder suggests a

best guess for the Scale (Range) of an Axis but it is up to you to finally define the range. These settings can be done in the already known Axis-Tab of the Chart options, entering the minimum and maximum data point.

- **Alignment:** The order of numbers or dates on an axis is derived from the order – information of the Field it is based on, so you are free to use any of the grouping and sorting options available to achieve the sequence you need to get. In case you are using a DateTime data type on an Axis it is your choice weather you want to treat the data in a numeric way or to display it in the so called scalar mode as DateTime by (in scalar mode only one grouping is allowed !). In scalar mode you will find similar options to Excel allowing you to specify the Interval (Report Builder suggests one) and the side margins to apply.

6.5.9.5   3 - D Affects

A lot of Chart types give you the option to convert them into their three dimension brother by adding a Z-Dimension (depth) to the Chart. Like in Excel also in this place it is wise to think for a second if it really is needed to have three dimensions to display your data or if it´s just a graphical brushing up of the data. To convert a Chart into 3 – D right click with the mouse on the Chart, choose *Chart options* and on the *3D Effect tab* check the *Display Chart with 3-D visual effect* Checkbox.

If you use a 3 – D Chart you have the options to rotate horizontally and vertically by +/- 90 degrees (although the GUI accepts higher values they are resized to 90 when leaving the Window), define the perspective as well as the shading-algorithm used.

6.5.9.6 Chart Types

The Charts that are available in Report Builder client represent a subset of the big number of Chart types available in Microsoft Excel. As I do not want to fill many pages with information you are already familiar with I just give a list of the available Carts and assume you will look them up in Office.

- Area
- Stacked Area
- 100% Stacked Area
- Bar
- Stacked Bar
- 100% Stacked Bar
- Column
- Stacked Column
- 100% Stacked Column
- Hybrid Column/Line Charts: You can also create a chart that combines both columns and lines in a single chart. To do this, you create a column chart with multiple value series, then select the Plot data as line check box in the Format Data Series dialog box on one or more of the value series to display the data series as a line
- Doughnut
- Exploded Doughnut
- Line
- Smooth Line
- Pie
- Exploded Pie

6.6 Formulas and calculated Fields

Formulas allow the Information worker who designs a Report to combine data of different Attributes into one new generated field. Using Report Builder you have to click on *Report* → *new Field* or the *new field Icon* above the left-handed fields list and in the opening Dialog-Box you have to supply a new Field name and the Formula that defines the containing content itself. Each formula is generated in the context of an Entity (readable in the Caption of the Formula-Box), so the formula returns one value for each item in this entity. To do that one has the means of using:

- **References:** A Reference contains the information on which Fields you want to include in your Formula. It is possible to use native fields of the context-entity as well as Fields of different Entities and already calculated Fields.
- **Functions:** These are predefined Formulas that execute specific calculations and may require the input of parameters by the Information worker.
- **Operators:** These objects specify the operations you want to do on the values retrieved by the referenced fields. For a list of valid Operators in Report Builder client and the way these Operators work refer to Chapter 4.7.2
- **Constants:** A constant is a value that is not calculated (and in this way does not change in the Formula). Report Builder allows *True*, *False* and *Empty* to be used as Constants in Formulas.

Some of the Attributes you are presented in Report Builder client were built using a Formula (for example Aggregations) behind the scenes without the demand to edit these formulas by yourself. If you are interested in the underlying Formula or if you want to modify the Formula to some special demand (perhaps your business treats a specific type of data different in an aggregation than the standard would require) you can open up the Define Formula Dialog, drag the Attribute into the formulas field, right click on the Attribute and choose *Replace with Definition* to get the Object and its Formula.

One interesting note I would like to give is on the use on duplicate data. If you want to keep or remove duplicate rows of data in your

Formula depends on the business scenario you are about to solve, but Report Builder allows you to set both Options. By default Duplicates are not removed, so if you want to do that click on *Keep all Duplicates of* and in the opening Dialogue choose which Duplicates you want to remove.

The last point the Information worker has to keep in mind when defining Formulas is in which way an aggregation on the new generated Field should happen. Use Aggregate to here. By right clicking on of the formulas source-fields and choosing extend you have the possibility to define a filter that limits the data used in the calculation.

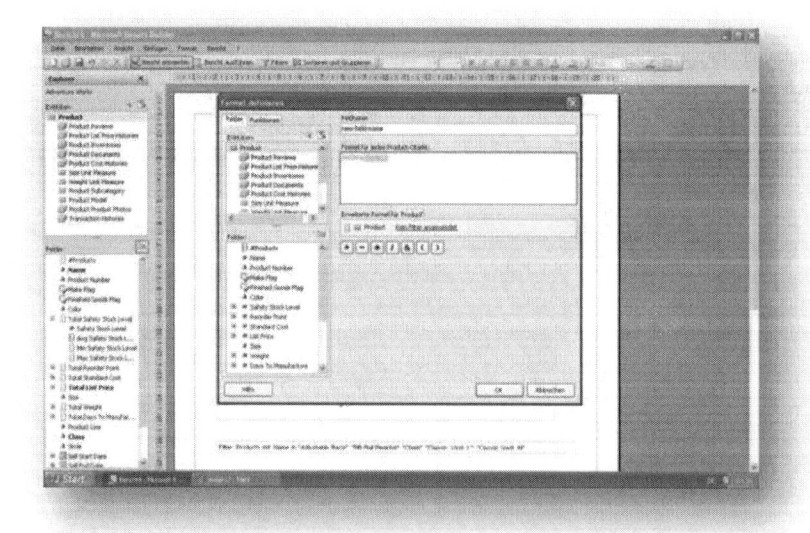

Image 17: extending a formula

6.7 Filtering data

A filter condition is a statement by which Report Builder client decides which data will be displayed in the generated Report or which data takes place in a calculation or Formula, limiting the rows used to those which meet the filter criteria.

To add a filter condition click on *filter* in the *menu* than drag a field from the fields-collection in the left handed pane of the filter dialog to the design-surface and a comparison operator and a filter condition. Report Builder supports, depending on the DataType of the field to filter on these operators

- **Equals:** This operator is usable on all types of data. Report Builder provides a List (which type is depending on the settings the developer of the Report Model designed) from which you can choose one entry.
- **In a List:** If this option is selected usually Report Builder shows all the available items to choose from in a List. The type of the List that is used is defined by the developer who designs the Report Model. Check all the values you would like to use in these criteria. Sometimes the List, built out of an Entity is not that user-friendly as it may consist of a big number of instances (if the entity is based on a large table) whereas only a few ones bring reasonable results when used in a Filter. To come around this fact you can create own Pre-filtered Lists to be used in this scenario. The definition of a Pre-filtered list is covered in Chapter 6.7.4
- **Greater then (or equals):** This operator is only available for numeric data and acts as expected as it does a numerical comparison between the data and the search condition which has to be entered in a textbox.
- **Less than (or equals):** This operator is only available for numeric data and acts as expected as it does a numerical comparison between the data and the search condition which has to be entered in a textbox.
- **From…To** acts as a combined operator acting like both of the above operators, delivering numeric data that lies in between the defined borders.
- **Contains:** This operator is only available for textual data. The text you enter in the provided textbox must be found in the searched attribute to qualify for data retrieval. For a developer this maps to a *like %string%* clause in SQL.

Every operator I described has a NOT prefixed version that operates as you might expect, it is the opposite way and returns the rows that do not meet the specified filter criteria.

One special case is to filter on are fields that contain empty cells or zero-length strings (in case of a text field). To filter out empty fields (in terms of database language on NULL values) use the IsEmpty operator, to get all the blank values (for textual data) out use the IsBlank operator. As it is a frequent request to combine these two by on OR, Microsoft does not require you to concatenate these two but delivered a preset combination already with the title IsBlankorEmpty.

If you are filtering on Date and Time values frequently you will not just have the demand to select one specific date, but to have relative date- and time filters (for example sales of the last 30 days). So Microsoft provides a set of those that are most needed date-range functions:

- **To Date...Month:** This relative filter returns data from the first day of the selected month to the current day (when the Report is executed).
- **To Date...Quarter:** This relative filter returns data from the first day of the selected quarter to the current date (when the Report is executed).
- **To Date...Year:** This relative filter returns data from the first day of the selected year to the current date (when the Report is executed).
- **Next (n)...Days:** This filter returns data raging from today plus the number of days specified in the filter condition.
- **Next (n)...Days (including today):** This filter acts as a variation to the previous one as it acts the same way, with the exception that today's data is also included.
- **Next (n)...Months:** This filter works like its day-variety before and returns data raging from this month plus the number o months provided.
- **Next (n)...Months (including this month):** Acts like the one before with the exception that the actual month is also included.
- **Next (n)...Years:** This filter works like its day and month variety before and returns data raging from this year plus the number of years provided.

- **Next (n)…Years (including this year):** Acts like the one before with the exception that the actual month is also included.
- **Last (n)…Months** Acts like its Next.. Counterpart but in a different direction on the timeline.
- **Last (n)…Months (including this month)** acts in the same way like its predecessor, with the exception that the data of the actual month is included.
- **Last (n)…Days** Acts like its Next.. Counterpart but in a different direction on the timeline.
- **Last (n)…Days (including today)** acts in the same way like its predecessor, with the exception that the data of the actual day is included.
- **Last (n)…Quarters** Acts like its Next.. Counterpart but in a different direction on the timeline.
- **Last (n)…Quarters (including this quarter)** acts in the same way like its predecessor, with the exception that the data of the actual quarter is included.
- **Last (n)…Year** Acts like its Next.. Counterpart but in a different direction on the timeline.
- **Last (n)…Years (including this year) acts** in the same way like its predecessor, with the exception that the data of the actual quarter is included.
- **This…Month** returns data of the current calendar month based on the day the Report is executed.
- **This…Quarter** returns data of the current calendar quarter based on the date the Report is executed.
- **This…Year** Returns data of the current calendar year based on the date the Report is executed.
- **Same Last Year…Month** Returns data for all the days of the same month one year ago.
- **Same Last Year…Quarter** Returns data for all the days of the same quarter one year ago.

Out of the box the following date-value functions are provided:
- Today
- Now
- Yesterday

- Tomorrow
- First day of month
- First day of quarter
- First day of year
- Last day of month
- Last day of quarter
- Last day of year
- (n) days ago
- (n) months ago
- (n) years ago
- (n) days from now
- (n) months from now
- (n) years from now

To remove a filter you have to click on the Attribute filtered on in the Filter – design area and choose remove condition.

6.7.1 Filtergroups and complex filters

Filtering in Report Builder is not limited to a simple sequential filter operators concatenated with the two logical operators (and, or). In this place Microsoft allows you to define Filtergroups that can be concatenated with some more operators, I will describe after the definition of a Filtergroup. A filter group contains one or more filter conditions connected by the same logical operator. Grouping filter conditions helps refine the data returned when the filter is applied to the Report and makes it easier to maintain and understand the filter – settings. To add a Filtergroup navigate to the Dropdown-Button in the upper right area of the filter Window, click on it and select one of the operators by which you want to add a group.

- **Any of:** Any condition defined in the Filtergroup has to apply to deliver data back.
- **All Of:** All of the provided conditions in all Filtergroups have to apply to deliver data back.

- **None of:** This Option is the opposite of *All Of* as it only delivers data back that does not apply to all the provided filter conditions.
- **Not All of:** This Option is the opposite of Any Of as it delivers data that is not applying to one of the filter sets.

Inside a Filtergroup you can add filter conditions as described above, or another (nested) Filtergroup. The place where a new Filtergroup is placed when you click on the button is designated by active group (it gets a very decent highlighting), so make sure you have an eye on the design area prior to the Filtergroups selection.

Individual Filtergroups can be concatenated like filter conditions by using and/or.

You can change the type of a Filtergroup by clicking on the operator that is designating the title of the group and choosing another option. This is also the one and only place in which you have the option to get rid of a Filtergroup again as there is no other way (delete-key, dragging it somewhere) to dispose this element.

6.7.2 Filtering and Formulas

In Report Builder client you are not limited to filter on Attributes of an Entity that are directly bound to the underlying data source. In the same Interface you are also given the possibility to filter on calculated fields, no matter if they origin in the Report Model (expressions) or in Report Builder (Formulas). Just treat them like any other source for a filter.

Another interesting option Microsoft offers in this place is to have a Filter condition displayed and editable as a Formula. When clicking on a Condition like the Location in the image below you get a Formula-Popup Window that displays the Filter Condition as an editable Formula. After editing the Formula you no longer have a "classical" filter condition in this place but a Formula-like construct. This gives you great flexibility in creating your very specific filters, depending on all features the formula – interface provides.

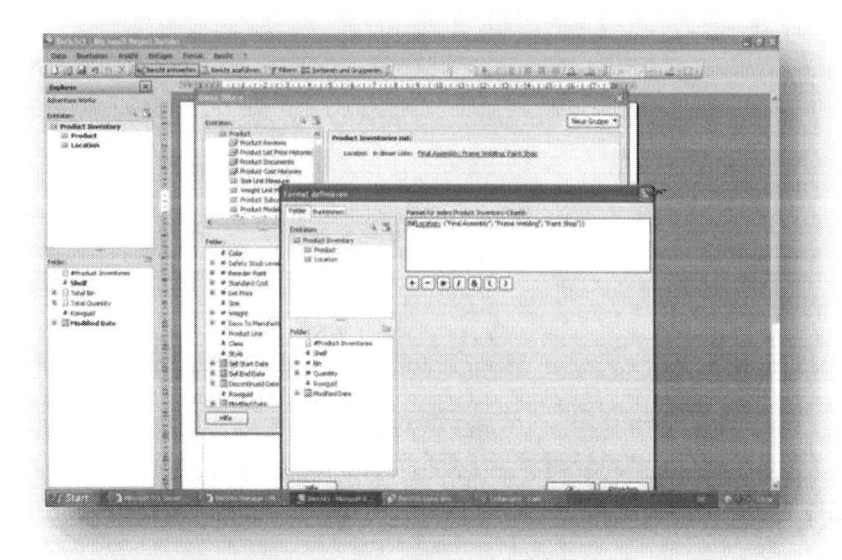

Image 18: Converting a Filter condition into a formula

6.7.3 Filtering at runtime

If you require the end users who consume the generated Reports to state Filter-parameters at the runtime of the Report you are generating in Report Builder this is possible, but gives you some limitations in Report management and Subscription as I will point out later.

To set such a condition (referred to as a prompt), enter the first parts of the Filter as usual, but instead of selecting or entering a filter-value right click the Mouse and select *Prompt*. To indicate that the Parameter is queried at runtime Report Builder shows a green question mark just before the filter condition. If you also entered a text or selected a value the Report will first run with these as a default and give the end user the possibility to change the settings in the next step. If no data is entered the end user is required to enter/select values right from the beginning.

6.7.4 Prefiltered Lists

If the out-of-the-box list of available instances of an entity to choose from would grow too big, you are prompted to create your own pre-filtered list when using the *In a List* operator. Using this pre-filtered list gives you the opportunity to limit the number of items displayed within a pre-populated list or to specifically compile a list meeting special demands if you intend to relay on user input for filtering. Then, just like with any other native list, you or the end user (in case of a prompt) can select which items to add to the filter condition.

When creating a pre-filtered list, keep in mind that you are not specifying your criteria to filter; you are simply limiting the criteria options available from which you or the end user can select the filter condition criteria. It is only a way to make potentially big and clumsy selection lists a bit more user friendly by applying some previous knowledge.

Prefiltered Lists show up a bit clumsy if they are used as a prompt in Report manager as it is displayed as a textbox containing the previous selected values. If the End-user wants to deselect an Item he or she has to delete it, adding is just possible by text, also other text is accepted. This type of unfriendly behaviour results out of the Report Model structure. The Report Model anticipates a textual list for a filter-condition and all report Builder does is supplying an interface to pretend you are working with a list. Unfortunately this approach is not absolutely well done, so make sure your users understand the way it works before you use it.

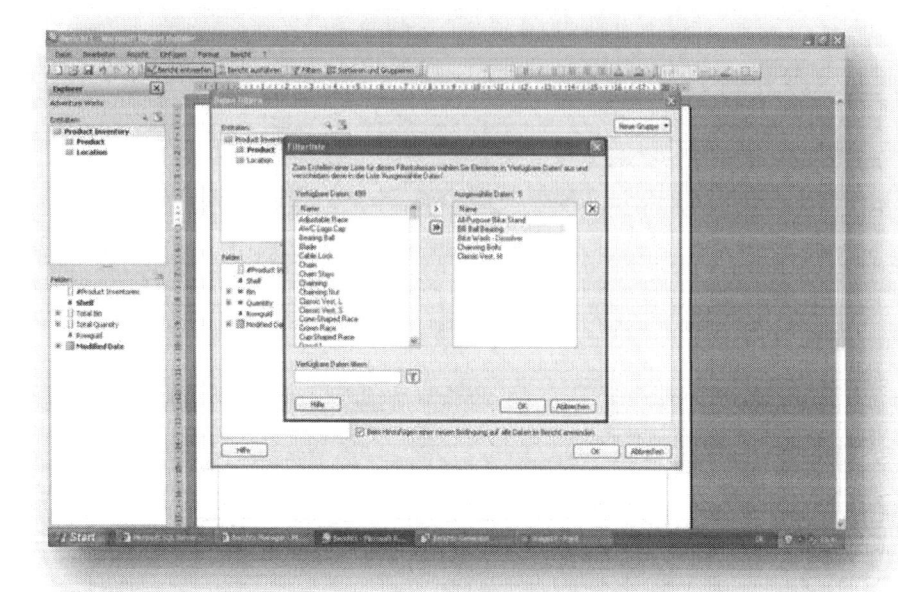

Image 19: designing a Prefiltered List in report Builder

6.8 Grouping

Groups are used in ad Hoc Reports to organize the data for calculation and displaying purposes. There is no limit in the number of groups a Report can contain. As soon as a Report contains aggregates and/or subtotals the groups gain a big importance. In the design surface you can see the Groups in a List or Matrix as Tabs on the according position. To get correct aggregations the way groups are ordered is from left (raw) to right. On the right side is the group with the highest level of details. If you are grouping on two axes using a Matrix it is also possible to nest these two levels of grouping. There are two groups distinguished in Report Builder:

- **Value groups.** Earns multiple rows
- **Entity groups:** earns one row

If you want to have multiple Groups you need to take a slightly uncommon approach to get the groups you need. For each group you want to achieve drag the whole entity into the design surface (you can delete the not needed Attributes later on) from the highest left) to the lowest group (right). This will result in groups you can see in the Tab above the Table or Matrix. Just dragging one Attribute of another Entity on the design surface will not yield you another group, it is just added to the group where you dropped it as an additional describing Field.

Keep in mind that a 1-to many role between the used entities might change your primary entity

To add a page-break between groups you have to use the Sort *and Group Menu*, choose the group and activate the Checkbox and chose the specific type when a page break is expected to happen.

6.9 Sorting

The data of a Report, no matter if in a Table, Matrix or Diagram can be sorted by the Information worker. To accomplish the task choose *Sorting & Grouping* in the Menu (or use CRTL + S); choose the group you want to sort, the Items to sort by and the direction. The Menu that provides you the items to sort by is built dynamically, so you are presented as many options as you have elements in your group. As the Interface already requires you to choose a Group first you have clear your mind that sorting only can happen on a group – level. To achieve a correctly sorted Report you will have to make sure you design it correctly using the information you got out of chapter 6.8.

One feature of ad-hoc report is that the Information worker, who creates the Report, has the option to enable an interactive sorting on Tables or Matrixes for the end users who consume it. To do that open the property of the Report you are working on in Report Builder client and enable user defined sorting. Once this is done you will see little clickable arrows pointing up or down in the headers of the mentioned objects. Clicking on these arrows sorts ascending or descending, dependant on the actual orientation of the arrow. Sorting on more than one column is also supported – use the Shift-Key to select more than one column to sort by and then choose the appropriate sorting. On word of caution from my side: As I pointed out earlier sorting only happens to the data in a group. This is clear for the end user if it is a summarizing Report using aggregates/visible groups. When generating a Report that does not obviously show groups it is very important that the Information worker makes sure the end user knows how the data is grouped, otherwise there will be complaints that the sorting does not work as expected.

6.10 Clickthrough Reports (aka as infinite drill-trough reporting)

Report Builder Reports provide an interesting and quite unique feature called infinite drill-trough reporting. In brief this means that every Entity of a Report can be the starting point for another Report accessing a deeper layer of data which also can act as starting point for another deep dive into the next layer of data and so on. This process can go on until you have no more logical path in your Report Model to follow, so Microsoft refers to it as literally infinite. The point I want to make is here that the ability which paths the consumer of the Report can follow is determined by the developer that designs and builds the Report Model.

This feature is only available in the Enterprise Edition of SQL Server 2005. If you are on another Edition you might encounter some suspect error Messages when trying to use this feature but the message behind is simply – use the right edition of SQL Server to get this functionality.

6.10.1 Temporary drill-trough Reports

These Reports are automatically created by Reporting Services (remember: only in Enterprise Edition) on the fly once you navigate to a single Entity or a list of Entities of a Report Model. Based on the information defined in the Report Model (Identifying Attributes and Default Detail Attributes) and the according Template, which cannot be changed (the Report represents a single Entity or a List of Entities) this Report is generated on the fly. One caveat is that you cannot change the style of these templates, not even their color.

If the generated Clickthrough Report does not fit your purposes and the limitation of a Report Model does not allow you to define it as you need it, you can define a predefined (static) Report, which is described in the next chapter.

6.10.2 Predefined (static) drill-trough Reports

If the Reports for Entities that Reporting Services designs for you on the fly do not fulfill your needs or if there are Reports in production already that show information related to a simple entity in a perfect way this option allows you to build a link to these and overrule the autogenerated ones (one exception – if the user does not have sufficient permissions to view the targeted Report he will be presented the autogenerated one).

As you are not just limited to Report Builder Reports this option gives you the possibility to use the rich Design - environment Report Designer provides as well as the possibility to consume different DataSources in one Report.

To archive this task take the following steps, assuming your Report Model is already published to the Report Server which needs to be the Enterprise Edition:

- Create a Report for the desired entity in Report Builder based on the same Report Model as the *parent* Reports.
- Publish the Report to the Report Server
- Use SQL Server Management Studio to navigate to the Report Model on the Report Server, right click on the Report Model and choose *Properties*
- Navigate to the *Drilltrough-Reports* Page, locate the Entity you would like to link to a static drilltrough Report.
- Choose the SingelInstance and MultiInstance report you would like to provide and off you go.

6.11 Publish Reports

Like a classic Reporting Services Report, also Report Builder reports are saved in RDL format. When this RDL file is saved to a Reporting Server the process is called publishing a report.

Usually a Report is published when the creator of the report wants to run the report regularly (publish to MyReports if possible) or if the Report is to be shared with other members of the organization.

Not all .smdl files can be uploaded. If the file is missing data source view information, you will get an error when attempting to upload the file. Data source view information will be missing if you attempt to upload a .smdl file that has never been published to a Report Server before. Before publishing from Model Designer, the .smdl file and data source view are stored separately. During publication, data source view information is merged into the .smdl file. As a result, you should only upload a .smdl file that has been previously published to a Report Server, and then subsequently saved from the Report Server to the file system.

7 Security

When dealing with a Report Model and Report Builder environment there are a lot of components involved in the delivery of the complete solution and a lot of places where a developer and/or administrator can shape Security settings. At a first glance it might be misleading and you might get snowed under the possible options and their reach, but structured in a logical connected way I hope I can clarify how the Security settings work together.

7.1 Report Model Security

In the previous Chapters I outlined a lot of places to define some security information in a Report Model using the Model Designer environment. Once the Report Model is published to a Reporting Server the administrator of the particular Server can use SQL Server Management Studio to define Security Settings (permissions) on a number of objects of a Report Model. Model Item security is off by default, after the administrator enabled model item security, it is possible to create Role assignments on the following specific nodes in the Report Model:

- **Securing the Folder Namespace:** As with all items that are stored on a Report Server, you can define item - level role assignments that determine whether a user can view or manage a Report Model. Users who have the permission to view a Report Model can see it in the folder hierarch of the Report Server, read a limited amount of information about the Report Model in the General properties page (for example, when it was created or modified), and query the Report Model by clicking through links in any ad hoc Report that uses the Report Model as a data source. Users who have permission to manage a Report Model can delete, rename, and update the Report Model. Typically, model management tasks also require the ability to publish new Report Models, but the ability to do that is actually conveyed through role assignments on folders, where the folder role assignment determines whether users can add items to it. Users who have permission to view a published model cannot open it directly to view its

contents or download it to the file system. At run time, all interaction with the report model is through the report that uses it
- **Folders & Perspectives:** These objects which are used to give a Report Model a structure or make it easier usable are not securable objects per se. A whole perspective or folder can't be secured, but the items that are contained in one of these structures can be secured using Model Item Security.
- **Model Item Security** allows the developer or administrator to control access for users to specific parts of a Report Model. A Report Model is represented as a hierarchical structure that includes a root node, Entities, Roles, and Attributes as nodes. When the Report Model is viewed in Management Studio, the administrator can browse this hierarchical structure and specify role assignments at different levels. It is possible to specify role assignments on the root node of a Report Model to control access to the entire Report Model (permissions are inherited), or on parts of a Report Model to vary access permissions on selected branches. The hierarchy supports the inheritance of security settings for items lower in the tree structure. Model item security is transparent to the user. If a user does not have access to a particular branch of the model hierarchy, that portion of the model is not presented to the user in the report (it is not returned by the getuserModel function of the Reporting Server). Using model item security, the Report Server modifies the query that is sent to the data source to exclude any portion of the model that is off limits to the user.

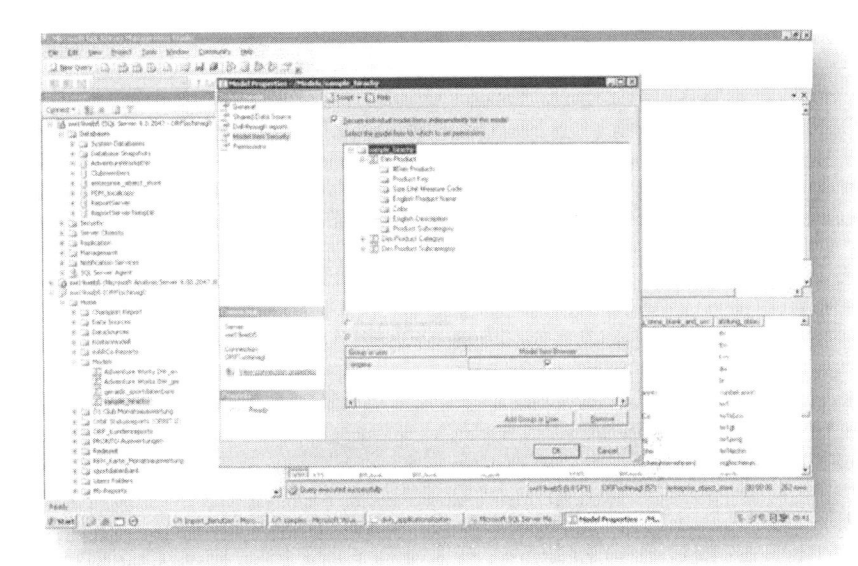

Image 20: Managing Model Item Security in Management Studio

- **Security Filters:** These objects that were described earlier in this book allow the implementation of row-level security. The filters themselves do not implement a security – limitation when defined, but they are also objects that can be secured by Model Item security. If a user does not have the sufficient permissions for a SecurityFilter he or she won't see the so defined data of the Entity's containing this filter in the generated Reports.
- **Opaque Expressions:** These Attributes that are based on Expressions are a convenient way to do some calculations using secured values that are not visible for the information worker and end user to be summed up in a visible Expression. This approach is recommended if you have, for example to deliver a report on sales-numbers, but the information workers and end users may not see the individual sales records. So defining a summary Expression on this data and hiding the source data solves the problem.

7.2 Report Builder client Security

For the usage of Report Builder client by the information worker and the consumption of the created Reports by the end user another set of permissions applies.

- **Accessing Report Builder Client:** To access Report Builder over the Report Manager website the targeted users need to be associated on the system level to a security group that has assigned the *Execute Report definition* Right. This can either be done by adding the Group to the Administrators or System Users Role (a Standard Role Reporting Services creates on install). The association has to take place on the system-level as the link to Report Builder is contained in the root level of Reporting Services hierarchy. Also this group needs to be associated with an Item Level Role called *Report Builder* (described in Chapter 7.2.1) to have the permission create Reports, load Reports view and navigate the Report Model.
- **Role based security on a Report Model:** Users who have the right to view a Model can see it in the Report Manager folder hierarchy as well as in Report Builder, read some general information (Description, Create Time) an use it in any Report that is based on this Model (assuming you have the Right to see the report). A read Permission on the Report Model also allows a user to build a classical Report in Report Designer on it. Users who have permission to manage a model can delete, rename, and update the model. The ability to publish a Report Model is actually conveyed through Role assignments on folders, where the folder Role assignment determines whether users can add items to it.
- **Securing Items in a Report Model:** How to accomplish that task is described in chapter 7.1 For the information worker the effect is that he only sees the items the developer or administrator wants him to see based on his Entity or membership in Active directory Groups.

- **Accessing Data:** The permission which part of the data a user of a Report gets delivered is depended on the Model Security and described in that place.
- **Connection permissions**: Besides this permission keep in mind that also a Report Model itself can act as a DataSource for a Standard Report. A user who accesses this report needs the permission to use the Report Model.
- **Database Security:** To use this Security layer you have to make sure that the connection to the database is done using Windows Integrated Security, so the Users credentials are really used to access the data. If the user is not allowed to access particular Tables or Columns there is an Access Denied Error returned to the Report. But be aware that the caveat of this approach might limit the usability for the user as at some point during his work he might be confronted with a real error message.

7.2.1 Report Builder Role

The Report Builder role is a predefined role of reporting Services that includes permissions for loading reports and as viewing and navigating the folder hierarchy. The following list describes the sub permissions that are included in the Report Builder role definition.

- **Consume reports:** This Role allows the user to read report definitions from the Server.
- **View reports** allows the user to view the properties of reports and run them
- **View resources** allows to view resources and their properties.
- **View folders** allows a user to navigate the folders and view the contents of folders.
- **View Models** allows the user to view Report Models, use them as a DataSource for Reports, either in Report Designer or in report Builder as well as to run queries against the Model for data retrieval.
- **Manage individual subscriptions** allows the creation and management of report-subscriptions.

The Report Builder role can be modified to suit special needs. The recommendations are generally the same as for the Browser role: remove the "Manage individual subscriptions" task if it is not planned to support subscriptions, remove the "View resources" task if resources are not to be seen, and keep "View reports" task and the "View folders" tasks to support viewing and folder navigation.

The most important task in this role definition is "Consume reports", which allows a user to load a report definition from the report server into a local Report Builder instance.

7.2.2 Model Item Browser Role

This is the generic role to browse the Report Model to see which objects are available. Assigning someone to this role is the easiest way to give someone full read access without allowing management or modification of report items.

8 Report Management

8.1 The Reporting Services Webservice

All the functions of Reporting Services are exposed via a Webservice (http://yourserver/ReportServer/Reportservice2005.asmx?wsdl). This Webservice contains a number of properties and functions. In the subsequent text the functions, which are related to Report Models or Report Builder are explained with their impact on the Reporting Services System. For the syntactical details and the needed parameters refer to Books Online.

- **CreateDataSource:** This function allows the administrator of a Report Server to define a DataSource in a given folder, no matter which type the connection is based on. For a code example go to 4.9.3
- **CreateModel:** This function allows the uploading the contents of an SMDL file to the Report Server. For a code example go to 4.9.2. The return value of this function is an array of warning messages that result of the Report Models validation. If the upload fails an exception is thrown. Doing the creation of a Report Model also modifies the ModifiedBy and ModifiedDate of the folder the Report Model is created in.
- **GenerateModel:** This function accepts a shared DataSource that has to be an OLAP or SQL Server Source as a parameter where it builds a Report Model on. The resulting Report Model gets the IsGenerated property set to true. Keep in Mind that the Report Model is generated using the credentials specified in the shared DataSource. If this DataSource uses Windows integrated Security the resulting Report Model for different users who create the Report Model may look different.
- **GetModelDefinition:** Returns the whole Report Model as a Base 64 encoded byte array to the client. This function is involved when you script/download the Report Model from the Server.

- **GetModelItemPermissions:** Returns a XML structure in a string, which describes the permission set for a given item of a Report Model for the user who is requesting the information.
- **GetModelItemPolicies:** This function returns an array of policy objects that describe the groups and their Roles that are associated with the requested item. If no item ID is
- **GetUserModel:** This function returns a Base 64 encoded Byte array representation of the semantic part of the requested Report Model or Perspective, stripped down to the items the user of Report Builder has the sufficient permissions on.
- **InheritModelItemParentSecurity:** Deletes the policies associated with a model item and causes the model item to inherit the policies from its parent. Keep in mind that you have to supply an Item ID (as the root level has no parent it could inherit security settings from). Also be aware that this function also changes the security settings for all child nodes of the supplied Item.
- **ListModelDrilltroughReports:** Lists the drilltrough reports associated with a given Entity of a Report Model the user has read-permissions on.
- **ListModelItemChildren**: Returns an array of model item child elements of the provided Item. If no Item is defined the function takes the root level of the Report Model. This function is used to get the associated Items for the Navigation in Report Builder client.
- **ListModelPerspectives**: This function lists all perspectives of a Report Model available to the information worker. If no Model name is defined in the consumption of the function, Report Server delivers all Report Models (respective the standard- Perspective of the Report Model) that a user has permissions on are delivered. This is the function that fills the initial selection in report Builder, where the information worker is required to choose a Report Model to work with.

- **RegenerateModel**: Updates an existing model based on changes to the data source schema. A word of caution in this place – the regeneration of a Report Model may break existing Reports based on this Report Model if Entities are removed or renamed.
- **RemoveAllModellItemPolicies**: Deletes all policies associate with model items in the specified model. After this function has been executed all Items of the Report Model are accessible for all users.
- **SetItemDatasources**: Sets the data sources for an item in the catalogue. Be aware that although the function allows the input of a array of Data Sources it is only possible to insert one single Data Source for Report Models. The definition of a DataSource for a Report Model does not allow a Source that is based on another Report Model as Source. Data Sources that request a prompt (for credentials) are also not valid for Report Models in this function.
- **SetModelDefinition**: This function replaces the definition for a specified Report Model on the server. The model ID of the submitted byte array the represents the Report Model must match the ID of the existing model it is replacing, or an rsModelIDMismatch error is returned.
- **SetModelDrilltroughReports**: Associates a user defined drill-through reports with an item of a Report Model. If an Entity has no associated Drilltrough Report defined Reporting Services will direct the user to a dynamically defined Report.
- **SetModelItemPolicies**: Sets (replaces) the security policies on a supplied model item. At least one policy has to be supplied; otherwise the function will return an error.

8.2 The Reporting Services Database

This topic covers the Reporting Services database from a Report Model and Report Builder client perspective. I will not cover all the internals of the Reporting Services Database, but I want to go into the details of tables and procedures that have some influence on ad hoc Reporting. These Objects will give you the possibility to add some extension you might need (described in Chapter 9) or to do some reporting on this Database for regulatory Reasons.

8.2.1 Database – Tables

The description of the Tables is intended as a piece of information. It is strongly recommended not to change any setting directly in the database as it might result in an unusable Reporting Services database. To give you the possibility to have a look on these objects without hazard I have built a report Model on the database, which is available as ssrs_model in the samples. If you really have to edit the database be sure to backup it first in case it gets corrupted.

- **Catalog:** This table contains all Items that are available on the particular Report Server. The content itself is stored in a Binary column, but some of the Metadata might be of interest. The Type column gives you an indication which object a row of data is. 1 stands for a folder, 2 for a report – no matter if it was built by Report Designer or Report Builder, 5 stands for a DataSource and 6 for a Report Model
- **DataSource:** contains all DataSources stored on the Reporting Server. If you are curious – Report Model DataSources are indicated by a value of 19 in the flags column.
- **ModelDrill** contains the Information about a static or dynamic drilltrough report as described in chapter 6 already.
- **ModelItemPolicy:** If ModelItem Security is enabled the individual Rules resp. Permission sets (represented) as Policy this table contains one row for each object in the Report Model that is secured with a Policy.
- **ModelPerspective:** contains all perspectives of Report Models. One interesting observation in this place: Perspectives of relational Models have a GUID as the identifier, whereas Report Models that were built from a UDM Source are described by a namespace/name combination. If a Report Model

based on a UDM has been broken by renamed perspectives (and just renaming nothing else !) you have a chance to edit this field and bring the Report Model to life again.
- **Policies:** contains all the Groups that can have security permissions on an Object.
- **PolicyUserRole:** is an intersection table, which defines which user is member of which role under which policy.
- **Roles:** This Table contains the definition of defined Roles on Reporting Server and initially contains some of the standard – Roles Microsoft creates on install.
- **SecData** is a table that delivers additional Information to the permission tied to a policy by describing the users and groups in as well as some Information on ModelItems.
- **User:** This Table contains as its name indicates the credentials of the users and groups that carry some security permissions on the Reporting Server.

8.2.2 Used stored procedures

The description of the stored procedures is intended as a piece of information. It is strongly recommended not to change any of these procedures as you might lack support in case of failures and it is not sure that these procedures are not changed in a service pack. But sometimes it is a good idea to enhance these procedures to achieve better results in terms of tracing, manageability, extensibility and compliance. If you really have to edit the database be sure to backup it first in case it gets corrupted and test the changes extensively before you put it into production – and keep in mind that it is your risk to earn a corrupted an therefore unusable Report Database.

- **AddModelPerspective:** For an already existing Report Model this Stored Procedure allows the user to define a Perspective in the Report Server Database.
- **CreateObject** is the main stored procedure that creates every object that can be found in the Reporting Services Catalog. No matter what Item

is created, weather it is a DataSource, a Report Model or a report it is done by this Procedure. If you want to trace or manipulate the uploaded contend you will have to decode the binary data before you can handle it. But in terms of tracking compliance relevant changes this procedure is a good place to hook in. The enumeration of the types of objects created can be found in the previous chapter´s description of the catalog table.

- **DeleteAllModelItemPolicys** does as the name indicates a deletion of all Policies based on the Items of a report Model. Interesting in this place is that the procedure is not called using the identifier of the Report Model as a parameter but by using the Path of the Report Model
- **DeleteDrillThroughReports** removes the definition of a Report (a Catalog Item) as a target on drilltrough for a specific Report Model Item (in particular for an entity).
- **DeleteModelItemPolicy** allows you to remove on Policy on a particular Item in the reporting Services database. Other than the all – variety this procedure accepts the Identifier of the affected report Model.
- **DeleteModelPerspectives**: This Stored procedure deletes all perspectives belonging to one Report Model specified. If you redeploy a Report Model with changed perspectives first of all these are deleted using this stored procedure an then added by AddModelPerspective. As there is no Update – procedure in this place an update also is done using delete and then recreating the Perspectives.
- **DeleteObject**: works in the same way as I described it in the Perspectives already. Any re-deployment involves the delectation and recreation of the object handled.
- **GetDrilltroughReport**: delivers the associated Drilltrough report (if existing) for an Item of a

report Model by taking the path of a report Model and the Name of an Item as parameters.
- **GetDrilltroughReports** acts in the same way as the procedure above, with the exception that it takes the identifiers of the Report Model and the Item as inputs.
- **GetModelDefinition** delivers the Content of a Report Model as a byte stream.
- **GetModelItemInfo** delivers Security Information for a Report Model Item as a byte stream as well as an XML-Output
- **GetModelPerspectives** returns a list of all Perspectives of a Report Model that the calling user has privileges to access.
- **GetModelsandPerspectives** delivers a combined list (tree-list) of Report Models and the contained Perspectives that a user is allowed to see. This is the procedure that is called by Report Builder to display the selection-menu to choose a source on the startup screen. So for example if you want to enhance the description Information displayed to the information worker or do some additional limitations in the Items returned you would have to edit this procedure.
- **SetAllProperties** is a procedure that gives the possibility to change the description and modification parameters of any catalog item by its path.
- **SetDrilltroughReports** gives the opportunity to enter a new drilltrough report for a particular report Model Item.
- **SetlastModified** acts as a subset of the SetAllProperties procedure as it just modifies modification date and user.
- **SetModelItemPolicy** defines new policies for Report Items

8.3 Transformation of report Builder Reports to Report Designer Reports

The Reports that are generated by Report Builder produce the same RDL file like standard reports with the only exception that they use a Report Model as data source. After it is published there is no difference between those two on the Reporting Server. A Report Builder Report can be opened by Report Builder client or Report Designer. As Report Designer has far more functionalities than report Builder it is usually not possible to open a report in Report Builder that was modified by Report Designer (see later chapters for this approach). From that point on this Report is referred as Standard Report.

8.4 Subscription

Subscriptions are only possible for Reports that can be run unattended by the Reporting Server. If the Report needs input by a user (called a prompt) it is not possible to define a subscription, unlike a Standard Report which can run on defined parameters. Be aware that enabling model item security causes all reports running against this Report Model to have user-dependent behavior which makes subscriptions impossible.

8.5 Building Report Designer Reports on a Report Model DataSource

A Report that is designed in Report Designer cannot just be based on a Number of DataSources (OLAP, ADO, etc) Reporting Services provides. A Report in this toolset may also be based on a defined on a published Report Model (with some limitations in the Workgroup Edition of SQL Server 2005). Once you open Model Designer (in Visual Studio 2005 or Business Intelligence Studio 2005) and start to build a new Report, in the dropdown list of the possible connections to build a DataSet on you will find an entry named "*Report Server Model*". Once you choose this entry a textbox requires the designer of the Report to enter a connection string in the format server=http:/MyReportServer/reportserver;datasource=/Models/Modelname. After providing your credentials to access the Report Model, the Query Designer opens.

The Query Designer embeds a modified version of Report Builder (delivering Navigation and Design-Surface) which is enhanced by the preview of the returned results (you do not get this information on the fly in Report Builder, but Report Designer allows you to call the data instantaneously). All other functions work as you will know them from Report Designer.

8.6 Editing a Report Designer – Report in Report Builder

It is not officially supported by Microsoft that an information worker opens a Report that was designed in Report Designer (Visual Studio 2005 or Business Intelligence Studio 2005) but it is possible with some trial and error attempts, if you design these Reports according to the following rules:

- The report may not contain any headers or footers
- The Report may not contain rectangles or Lists
- The report may only be built of a single data region matching with the three templates report Builder provides (table, matrix, and chart).
- The Report may not contain any Linked/Embedded Reports.
- The data region has to be bound to a Report Model Query (no other data source is allowed).
- You have to make sure the in the data region a group (including the Details group, which must always be present) exactly matches the groups in the query, both in number and sequence (left-to-right for table, rows then columns for matrix, category then series for chart).

The possible benefit of this approach is that you get Clickthrough-Reports generated once you save this reports in Report Builder.

But my recommendation in this place: if you need to combine the possibilities of report Builder and report Designer plan well and do the Report Builder task first and execute the fine-tuning in report Designer. This approach saves you from the hoping and praying that the way I lined out before works, as it is not assured it always does (especially with upcoming Service packs).

9 Tips & Tricks

This section lines out some solutions, ideas, tips and tricks for specific problems or usage scenarios in the Report Model & Report Builder client environment. I will not provide complete solutions or code-blocks as on the one hand I assume that you – the developers know how to fulfill these tasks in your environment and on the other hand the specific possibilities (in terms of security, editions etc) are so different that you will have to modify these ideas anyway.

9.1 Report Model Tricks

9.1.1 Version Management & other Metadata

As I described earlier Report Models carry a field for the version but in this release of the tools it is not updated automatically when a new version of the Report Model is built. If you want to add Information into the Report Model there are two possible approaches.

1. **Fake the ReportServer2005.asmx Webservice:** You can write your own Webservice that replaces the original Webservice provided by Microsoft and delivers additional functionality. This can be done in the following procedure, but keep in mind – this is not supported by Microsoft, any Service Pack may break this approach and if any failures happen you are on your own.
    1. Find and rename the ReportServer2005.asmx to another name
    2. Build your own Webservice in this place
    3. Make sure the Webservice you build has exactly the same signature as the one you renamed earlier
    4. For each function you don't want to change just interface the renamed Webservice
    5. For the SetModel Definition you can do some modifications. The Content of the Report Model is delivered as byte array to the Webservice, you have to convert it into an XML-type, then use XQuery to locate the nodes you want to change, use some

logic to define the values you want to set, set the values transfer back into a byte array and call the function of the renamed Webservice.

2. **Modify the CreateObject stored procedure** on the Report Database is also a possible approach which is easier in terms of needed changes but requires more experience in T-SQL. Keep in mind that this stored procedure likely changes when a Service Pack is applied so make sure to save and reapply the modifications you did.
    1. Find and open the stored procedure
    2. Limit the following modifications only to uploaded Report Models (type equals 6).
    3. Define a XML variable
    4. Convert and load the content of the varbinary input parameter into the variable
    5. Use XQuery to locate and modify the nodes that you would like to update
    6. Reconvert the XML into a byte array and move on in the procedure.

9.1.2 Calculated fields

If the existing fields (entities) do not meet your demand, or the demand of the Information worker you create the Report Model for you can define own fields with using all the possibilities expressions supply.

9.1.3 Handling intersection Table (or how to handle m:n relationships)

Quite frequently in creating a Report Model on a classical OLTP database you are confronted with a many-to-many relationship. According to Codd´s Rules this logical reference is technically solved using an intersection Table and two foreign key constraints.

I assume you already know, an intersection Table contains no information besides the abstraction to persist an m:n relationship. So usually this structure carries no information that is of use for the Information worker and would just confuse them when using the Report Model to create the

Reports. The following approach shows you as a developer who builds report Models how to deal with this situation.

Assume we have 3 Tables; X and Z are the two entities that are connected in such a relationship using the intersection Table Y. If you autogenerate the Model you will get the following objects:
- An Entity for X
- An Entity for Y
- An Entity for Z
- One Role X → Y and vice versa
- One Role Z → Y and vice versa

Now it`s time to tweak the model in the following way:
- The Role X → Y is renamed to X → Z to reflect the correct direction it will stand for in Report Builder once you are done with this task.
- The Role Z → Y is renamed to Z → X to reflect the correct direction it will stand for in Report Builder once you are done with this task.
- Set the *expand Inline* property to true on the Roles Y → X and Y → Z (these are the reveres roles of the both you modified a step earlier)
- Add the Role Y → X to the HiddenFields collection of the renamed Role X → Z. This results in the Role Y → X not being displayed when the user navigates using the X → Z Role (remember the Role itself navigates to the intersection Entity Y, but the contents of Z are expanded inline).
- Add the Role Y → Z to the HiddenFields collection of the renamed Role Z → X This results in the Role Y → Z not being displayed when the user navigates using the Z → X Role (remember the Role itself navigates to the intersection Entity Y, but the contents of X are expanded inline)
- Finally the *Hidden property* of the Y Entity has to be set to true, as well as for Y´s Attributes. Now the intersection Entity (Y) is no more visible for the Information Worker, with one exception – it can be accessed in the Formula - Dialog.

9.1.4 Handling the MultiRoles Problem

It is a common scenario in OLTP systems that two Tables are related in more than one ways. For example in an order-handling System the customer Table and the address Table might be joined in multiple places as there may be more than one address – fields in the customers Table (like delivery address, billing address, technical contact,..) referencing the address Table. The Data Model might look similar to following

If you have the associated foreign keys defined the Report Model Generation Wizard will detect the one-to-many relationship from order to address and create an OptionalMany Role from Customer to Address, although we know that it is an optional 1:1 Reference. This behavior is not what you might want to achieve from a usability Role (the generated Roles would be usable but the information worker has to make address the primary Entity of the report), so here comes an approach for a better solution:

- **Enhance the Main Table** (in our case it's the customers Table) with calculated fields for each type of address. These Fields should be constants, it´s up to you if you want to do it with text constant (PRI, BIL, DEL) or if you want to use numeric identifiers. From a performance standpoint I would recommend using numeric identifiers. It is also up to you in which place you want to do that step, perhaps it´s depending on your influence over the system. These calculated fields may be added defining a View in the Source Database, or in the DSV defining a named query or adding calculated fields there.
- Defining a **unique constraint on the main Table** (in our case it´s the customers Table) tends to be a bit trickier, as the DSV – Editor does not allow defining unique constraints on non Primary key Columns. So open up the DSV-file in an XML – editor and find the primary key constraint in the orders Table. Insert a copy of it after it and set msdata:Primarykey = "false". Then add the Customer ID (the primary key) and the address-type. This step makes sure the Report Model generation Wizard knows that each

address-type may only show up once for each customer.
- As next step you **create/enhance the relationships** in the DSV from the main Table to the related Table (in our case the address Table). For each relationship between the two Tables enhance the Join – definition by a clause to limit it to the identifier of the generated Column in point 1
- **Create Roles** in the Report Model from Customer to Address, binding the on the previous generated relationships.

9.1.5 Evaluating the group – membership of a Report user

It is a frequent requirement to define some properties of a Report in Report Builder based on the information whether a user belongs to a given Active directory group or not. Unfortunately the GETUSERID function is the help Microsoft provides, so it seem there is no way to access the Group Membership information.

But using some of the features of SQL Server 2005 you can get this information into the Report Model (just in a Report Model based on a relational SQL Server 2005 database) using the following approach:

- Define a Table in the database the Model is based on that consists of two Columns (userid/string, ingroup/boolean and group name/string). Define the userid (optional userid and Group name) as Primary Key and insert a dummy-row into the Table so it is not empty.
- Create a Table-Valued User defined function that accepts two input-parameters (userid and group name) and returns a dataset that has the same structure as the previous generated Table. Deploy this UDF to the Database you are using and give the account report Builder will use to access the database the permissions to execute it.
- Define an instead of Trigger on the Table that evaluates the where clause of a select-statement that is executed against the database. If there is no where –

clause, which is the case when the Table is evaluated when it is entered into the DSV or the Report Model is created, then the dummy-row should be returned. If a userid and a group name are contained in the where clause then the previous generated SQLCLR function should be executed with the parameters.

- Enter the Table to the DataSource View (the data that will be evaluated is the entered dummy – row)
- Generate the Report Model using this Table. This will earn you an Entity with three Attributes (userid, ingroup and the name of the group)
- Define a Security Filter on the Entity that limits the userid Column of the Table to GETUSERID and the group name of the Table to a defined String (the group you want to check against). So this is the place where we force the semantic query engine to enter e where-clause to the generated query. Acting in that way will return a Table-structure that can be used for further purposes like filtering etc in the report Model.

9.1.6 The generated SQL/MDX Code of the Report Model Engine

For technically interested people sooner or later there grows the interest what kind of SQL – Statements Report Builder creates for a given report.

The easiest Solution (if you have the appropriate permissions on the targeted database) is to capture the generated SQL-Commands using SQL Profiler.

If you need to trace the generated Statements at the Reporting Server (not at the targeted database) it is required to modify the web.config file at the Report Server. You will have to locate the node named RStrace and identify the following statement:

<add name="Components" value="all, RunningJobs: 3, SemanticQueryEngine:**2** …etc and change the number 2 to 4. After you run the report you will find the generated set of SQL-Queries in a logfile located at: ..\Reporting Services\LogFiles\ReportServer_timestamp.log.

When you review the statements in this logfile they might not look like you expect them.

The first statement to give is that the selection and filters are totally independent, so selecting a particular field to display in the Report Builder Report will never reduce the rowset that is returned back. Technically speaking you will find left outer joins instead of the inner joins you might expect.

As a second specifica, the row Identity of the returned resultset is totally inviolate, that means no field may be added that would change the Identity of the rows in a group.

9.2 Report Builder Client Tricks

9.2.1 Launching Report Builder from a custom application

Regardless of the technique you might use, you're basically going to be hitting the URL http://Server/reportserver/reportbuilder/reportbuilder.application in the one or other way.

- **Winforms with the current logged on user**: In an application you have to start Internet Explorer, using Use System.Diagnostics.Process.Start with the URL of Report Builder as a parameter like in the C# sample:

```
System.Diagnostics.Process.Start("IExplore.exe", "http://localhost/reportserver/reportbuilder/reportbuilder.application")
```

- **Winforms using another Identity**: You can still use the Process.Start command, but you will have to make use of some members that are new in .NET 2.0 to specify the credentials. The Sample demonstrates how to run Internet Explorer under a different User account.

```
ProcessStartInfo startInfo = new ProcessStartInfo(@"c:\program files\internet explorer\iexplore.exe");
startInfo.UserName = "user goes here";
startInfo.Domain = "domain goes here";
startInfo.WorkingDirectory = @"c:\program files\internet explorer";
```

```
System.Security.SecureString sS = new System.Security.SecureString();
sS.Clear();
sS.AppendChar('P');
sS.AppendChar('a');
sS.AppendChar('s');
sS.AppendChar('s');
sS.AppendChar('W');
sS.AppendChar('o');
sS.AppendChar('r');
sS.AppendChar('d');
startInfo.Password = sS;
startInfo.Arguments                                                      =
"http://localhost/reportserver/reportbuilder/reportbuilder.application
";
startInfo.UseShellExecute = false;
startInfo.LoadUserProfile = true;
Process.Start(startInfo);
```

To use this solution, you need to have LoadUserProfile set to true for the used credentials or Report Builder can't get installed, because the ClickOnce cache is located in the UserProfile, so if you don't load the Profile, Internet Explorer does not know where to store the application.

- **Webform using the authenticated user**: This is a simple trick, you can use any technique you want (Link, JavaScript, ..) to navigate to http://yourServerName/reportserver/reportbuilder/reportbuilder.application

- **Commandline**: It is possible to launch Report Builder client by command line, but be aware that this feature is not supported by Microsoft and may not work on upcoming service packs.

  You just have to execute ReportBuilder.exe and specify the Server to connect to by using /s=yourreportserver (optional adding "/myreport" or "/model=modelname") as described in Chapter 6.1)

9.2.2 Enhancing the Report during publishing

To enhance an ad hoc Report during the publishing process (for example adding a company logo or a disclaimer by default) I do recommend a similar approach to the one already described in Chapter 9.1.1 dot 2, with the only exception that you have to use typ=4 as a filter to target Reports. But be advised that the reporting Services database does not make a difference between Standard reports and ad Hoc reports, so you have to test it on your own.

9.2.3 Retrieving images that are not inside the database

One common scenario of application designs that store images in the file system and only keep the path to the particular file in the database. The applications that use the database do the job of retrieving the image for the given path. If you build a Report Model on this database you obviously only get the path and not the content of the file.

If you are using a SQL Server 2005 database a possible solution is a SQLCR user defined function that takes the path as an input parameter and delivers the content of the file as binary array (resp. varbinary). Writing one function for this purpose is easy (5 Lines of code using the System.IO namespace). Using a named query you can replace the table in the DSV-designer and get all the content.

The shortcomings of this approach show up in two areas

- The performance of this solution is not really appealing as the database server goes out to the file system for each row returned.
- You need a lot of privileges and permissions on the database server (not every DBA allows you to use SQLCLR)
- It may be quite complex to configure the needed security permissions, you have to make sure the process SQL Server is running under can access the files.

9.2.4 Using RDL expressions in Report Builder

In a Textbox (not in a table or matrix cell !) you have the possibility to use some RDL – Expressions. This approach allows you for instance to show the execution-time for a report or the Parameters selected by the consumer of the Report. This is an undocumented feature so it is not sure it will work in the same way after the next Service packs. Also there is no GUI or graphical support for the Input.

If you want to use this feature I do recommend to pre-build these RDL-Expressions in a Report Designer Report and use these tested and working expressions as a blueprint. Once again remember – not every expression works so you have to test it on your own.

To use an expression enter a = into the textbox and afterwards the expression itself. For example:

- To get the execution date use =String.Format("Date: {0:MM/dd/yyyy}", DateTime.Today)
- To get the selected value of a parameter use =String.Format("The value of the parameter is : {0}", Parameters!usedparameter.Value). The caveat in this approach is that you do not get a display of the name Report Builder gives the parameter, you have to guess it (usually it is the name of the field prompted as filter condition) or dig around in the RDL-file to get the name.

9.3 Report Management Tricks

9.3.1 Building a Report Model on a Reporting Server Database

Regulatory demands sometimes require you to give some users access to the data stored in the Reporting Services database. This a hazardous task that should be strictly avoided but using a Report Model can make your life easier and more save as an administrator. By supplying a Report Model that only displays what is save to display, giving some enhancements and making readability easier gives those who need to retrieve data out of this system a great experience. Additionally you can be sure to have a tool that only has read-access on the Database.

To give an impression I did that job already on the Items in the reporting Services database that have some logical connection to Report Models (sample ssrs_model). It is easy to add additional tables; the only thing you need to explore is references (not all references are defined as foreign key in the database) and primary keys (they are sometimes missing). By defining these structures in the DSV you should get a good and fairly useable Report Model.

9.3.2 Using Visual Studio 200 Team Edition to Stress test your Report Server

When designing Ad – hoc Reports, the information worker does not have access to the generated queries that are needed to populate the Report, neither does the administrator. On the one hand this fact gives the information workers some independence from the IT department and lessees the possibility of fraud and errors, but on the other hand there is a risk that the queries generated by Report Builder are very complex and demanding or, especially when doing Clickthrough-Reports, return a mass of data.

These indications might prevent you as an administrator to permit Ad-hoc reporting on productive Databases.

If you need your users to access this data frequently it is a good practice to instantiate a performance testing process of the generated Report before it is deployed into production.

In this chapter I will line out how to accomplish this task using Visual Studio 2005 Team Edition.

To build a test-solution like the one I describe the Reports need to run without user-interaction (no Prompts).

1. Open VSTS and create a Test-Project using the New/Project window.
2. Create a Webtest. As Reporting Services renders its Reports using a web – interface the planned performance test will be based on a Webtest. To accomplish this task click on the project you created previously and choose add/Web test. Once the task is done an Internet Explorer Window pops up. At this point see the Recording-Menu in the left part of the window. In the Address Bar enter the URL of your Report Server you plan to test. One trick to avoid an rsExecutionError that results of Reporting Service´s Session-states is to suppress the Reports Toolbar using &rc:Toolbar=false (remember: we are talking

about Reports that do not need user interaction). A complete URL might look like http://yourserver/ReportServer/Pages/reportviewer.aspx?peportname&rc:Toolbar=false After hitting Enter the Report is loaded and this action is recorded as a blueprint for the test-playback. You can repeat this step as long as you want to with different reports you want to have included in this test run.

3. By hitting the Stop Button in the left handed recording Menu (Web Recorder) you end the recording of actions. If you like to run the whole recorded sequence now to validate all Reports you need are in you can use the Run-test Command in the Tests menu. At this point be advised that if you need to do more sophisticated Tests (simulating user input, test different rendering formats,...) you will have to code Unit Tests in VB.NET or C#.

4. The next step we want to take is to create a Load-test out of the earlier defined sequence of Report consumptions. To do that right click on the project in the solution – explorer again and choose add/Load test and you are welcomed by a wizard. First you have to define the usage-pattern and then you have to choose which recorded Web tests are to be run in the Loadtest you are creating. I recommend to us the Webtest we recorded in Point 2. In this place you could also choose a Unit test if you have more specific needs. In the next step you can define the Browser and network simulations that are to be applied to this Loadtest. The selection of the counters VSTS should monitor is a very important step as you now have to define which measures of the Reporting Server you are interested in to define the degree of performance to test.

5. A good practice to collect the Test-Results the Loadtest will generate is to create a Database for these Results. To do this locate the file loadtestrepository.sql in ../Visual Studio8/common 7/ide, open it in Management Studio, connect to a database server you have the privileges to create a

database on and execute the file to create the database. Once this is done step back to VSTS and select Administer Test Controllers in the Test Menu. In this place you have to enter the connection string to the database you created earlier on.

6. Now run the test by selecting the Run command. Now you can monitor the selected Counters live as well as the collected data is written into the database.

Index of images and figures

Image 1: Schema of Report Builder Components 11
Image 2: Structural Schema for Report Model generation 19
Image 3: Structural Schema for Report Builder usage 20
Image 4: Start page of the Report Model generation wizard 26
Image 5: The Model generation interface for a UDM Structure. 31
Image 6: generalised UML – Diagram of the Report Model structure 33
Image 7: Report Generation Wizard asking for the Culture – settings. 36
Image 8: Report Builder showing an EntityFolder 39
Image 9: Display of Perspectives in Report Builder 42
Image 10: Expression Builder GUI 74
Image 11: Start button for Report Builder client (localised in German: Berichts-Generator) 90
Image 12: selecting a Report Server in Report Builder client SP2 94
Image 13: Data Navigation in its initial state 96
Image 14: Data Navigation in its tree – state 97
Image 15: Data Navigation in its tree – state showing the extended Explorer 97
Image 16: frozen column in Report Builder client 113
Image 17: extending a formula 120
Image 18: Converting a Filter condition into a formula 126
Image 19: designing a Prefiltered List in report Builder 128
Image 20: Managing Model Item Security in Management Studio 135

Index

A

Active directory group 152
Active Directory Group 81
Active Views 12
ad Hoc Reporting 11
ad hoc Reports 10
ADD 82
Adobe Acrobat 108
aggregatable Attributes 47
Aggregate 95
Alignment 117
Analysis Services 13, 30
anchored expression 73
AND 81
Attribute 27
authentication 16
auto-increment Columns 27
Auto-increment columns 27
Avg 95
AVG 76

B

Background 105
Background Color 110
Books online 53
Books Online 17, 37, 49, 76, 139
Boolean 95
Border 110
Business Intelligence Studio 2005 18
business key 27
Business Model 32
Byte 58
Byte [] 59

C

calculated fields 24, 151

calculations 78
cardinality 69
Category group 113
Cell 110
Char 58
Chart 90, 101, 105, 113
ClickOnce 92, 93
Click-once application 89
CLR-Type 58
Codd´s Rules 149
Commandline 155
CONCAT 83
Condition 125
Constants 119
Contains 121
Count 95
COUNT 76
Count - aggregate 27
COUNTDISTINCT 76
CSS-Positions 108
CSV 109
Cube 12, 44, 45, 48
culture 64
Custom Datasource 23

D

Data Marker 114
DataSource View 20, 24
Date 95
DATE 79
DATEADD 79
DATEDIFF 79
DATEONLY 79
DATETIME 79
Day 95
DAY 79
DAYOFWEEK 79
DAYOFYEAR 79
Decimal 58
DECIMAL 78

denormalization 51
de-normalization 71
denormalize 50
Design Surface 46
Diagram 110
Dimension 42, 43, 68
DIV – elements 108
DIVIDE 82
divisor 81
Double 58
Drilldown 103
Drilltrough 102
Dropdown 48
dropdown list 67
Dundas Charting 113

E

Entity 26
Entity group 128
EntityFolders 38
EQUAL TO 82, 83
Equals 121
Excel 101, 107
EXPONENTATION 82
Expression 64
expressions 53
extractions 78

F

Fact 68
Fields 119
filter condition 120
Filter description 104
FilteredList 49
Filtergroup 124
Filtergroups 124
filters 53
FIND 83
First 95
Fixed headers 102
FLOAT 78
Font 110
foreign key 25, 28, 52, 68, 149

format string 65
Forms Authentication 16
Formula 73
Formulas 119
freezing 112
From…To 121
Functions 119
Functions Tab 74

G

GDI+ 109
GETUSERCULTURE 80
GETUSERID 80
Greater then 121
GREATER THEN 82, 83
Grid 104
Gridlines 116
Group Membership 152
Groups 128
GUID 34, 44, 58

H

hidden Folder 39
hierarchy 50
HOUR 79
HTML 108

I

IF 77
II 17
Image 95
IN 77
In a List 121
index 69
infinite drill-trough 130
instead of Trigger 152
INT 78
Int16 58
Int32 58
Int64 58
Internet Explorer 89, 92
Intersection 70

intersection Table 149
IsBlank 122
IsBlankorEmpty 122
IsEmpty 122
IsGenerated 139

K

Key Performance Indicators 56

L

Label 114
Landscape 103
Last 95
Last (n)...Days 123
Last (n)...Months 122
Last (n)...Quarters 123
Last (n)...Year 123
LEFT 84
Legend 115
LENGTH 84
Less than 121
LESS THEN 83
LESS THEN OR EQUAL TO 83
list 127
List 48, 101, 128
Loadtest 159
logarithmic scale 116
logfile 154
logical keys 37
Logical Primary Key 42
Lookup 49
LOWER 84
LTRIM 84

M

Major 116
Management Studio 102
MandatoryFilter 49
many-to-many relationship 70
Margins 103
Matrix 90, 101, 105, 128
matrix layout 75

Max 95
MAX 76
MDX 12, 53
mean 76
Measure 42
Measure Group 43, 56
-Menu 89
MHTML 108
Microsoft Excel 110
Microsoft Office 110
Min 95
MIN 76
Minor 116
MINUTE 79
MOD 81
Model designer 37
Model Designer . 17, 18, 19, 22, 28, 35,
  37, 38, 40, 43, 44,
  45, 47, 48, 70, 73
Model Item security 135
Model Item Security 134
ModelItem 38
Money 95
Month 95
MONTH 80
MSDN-Library 80
MULTIPLY 83
MultiRoles 151

N

named Filter 66, 73
Named Queries 24, 26, 37, 42
Navigation 95
NEGATE 83
Next (n)...Days 122
Next (n)...Months 122
Next (n)...Years 122
non-anchored expression 73
NOT 81
NOT EQUAL TO 83
NOW 80
NULL 62, 76
Number 94

O

Office 107
OLAP 10, 12, 30
OLTP.. 41
Opaque Expressions....................... 135
Operators.. 119
OR 81, 122
Oracle 23

P

Page Orientation............................ 103
Page units 103
Paper Size 103
PDF.. 108
permissions.................................... 133
Perspective 93
physical model 32
Portrait.. 103
Prefiltered List 127
Preview 107
primary Entity 98
Primary Key..................... 26, 27, 42, 46
prompt.................................... 126, 127

Q

Quarter 95
QUARTER 80

R

RDL.. 100
RDL – Expressions 156
Reference.. 119
RegenerateModel........................... 141
Regulatory demands...................... 157
REPLACE.. 84
Report Builder client........................ 11
Report Item........................... 106, 110
Report Manager.................... 21, 29, 86
Report Manager Website 18, 89
Report Model................................... 10
Report Model generation Wizard... 25
Report Model Project................. 17, 22
Report Server Webservice 87
Report Template 100, 101
Reporting Portal............................... 21
Reporting Server 10
Reporting Services .. 10, 12, 13, 15, 16, 91, 94, 109, 131, 141, 153
Reporting Services Configuration tool...................... 15
ReportServer2005.asmx................. 148
RIGHT 84
role assignments 133, 134
Role based security 136
ROUND 81
Rowcount 104
row-level security.......................... 135
RTRIM.. 84

S

Same Last Year...Month 123
Same Last Year...Quarter................ 123
SByte 58
Scale 116
Search-Window................................ 74
SECOND.. 80
Security 55
Security Filter 55, 135, 153
security group 136
Security settings............................. 133
self-service Reporting 11
Semantic Model 22, 32
Semantic Query............................... 11
Semantic Query Engine 59
Series group 114
Server Totals 103
Sharepoint Integration 93
Single.. 58
SmartClient 21
SMDL . 19, 20, 31, 32, 35, 37, 40, 43, 53
SQL Profiler 153
SQL Server Management Studio... 18

SQLCLR	153
SQLCR	156
SSL	17
standard-deviation	76
STDDEV	76
STDDEVP	77
String	58
Submodel	40
subreport	102
Subscription	126
subscriptions	137
Subscriptions	146
SUBSTRING	84
subtotals	66
SUBTRACT	83
SUM	77
SWITCH	78
System Objects	24

T

Table	24, 90, 105
Table-Valued User defined function	152
Tahoma	110
TargeServer URL	87
TargetDataSouce	87
TargetModel	87
template	90, 93
templates	17
Text	94
TEXT	78
textbox	75
Textbox	110, 156
This…Month	123
This…Quarter	123
This…Year	123
Tick marks	116
TIFF	109
Time	95
Titlebox	104
To Date…Month	122
To Date…Quarter	122
To Date…Year	122
TODAY	80

Tooltip	45, 58, 68
totals	66
TRUNC	82
trust relationship	16

U

UDF	152
UDM	.10, 12, 30, 31, 38, 39, 41, 43, 44, 45, 48, 49, 53
UDT	42
UInt16	58
UInt32	58
UInt64	58
unique constraint	151
UPPER	84
usability	151
user defined sorting	129
User Sorting	102
User-defined-DataType	42
UTF-8	108

V

value Axis	115
Value group	113, 128
VAR	77
variance	77
VARP	77
VB Script	76
Version - Management tools	35
View	24, 42
Visual Studio	17

W

warning	70
Webform	155
Webservice	20, 139
Webtest	158
WEEK	80
Windows Authentication	16
Windows Integrated Security	137
Winforms	154

X

X – Axis 113
XML 109
XML Notepad 34
XMLSpy 34
XQuery 148

Y

Y-Axis 115

Z

Year 95
YEAR 80

Z

Z-Axis 115
Z-Dimension 117

1952122

Made in the USA